BUILD A BETTER
VEGETABLE
GARDEN

30 DIY PROJECTS TO
IMPROVE YOUR HARVEST

JOYCE RUSSELL

PHOTOGRAPHY BY BEN RUSSELL

FRANCES
LINCOLN

For Sam, Nick and Anna –
who like making things too!

Brimming with creative inspiration, how-to projects and useful information to enrich your everyday life, Quarto Knows is a favourite destination for those pursuing their interests and passions. Visit our site and dig deeper with our books into your area of interest: Quarto Creates, Quarto Cooks, Quarto Homes, Quarto Lives, Quarto Drives, Quarto Explores, Quarto Gifts, or Quarto Kids.

Build a Better Vegetable Garden

© 2017 Quarto Publishing plc

Text copyright © Joyce Russell 2017
Photographs copyright © Ben Russell 2017
Edited by Zia Allaway
Design by Becky Clarke Design

First published in 2017 by Frances Lincoln, an imprint of The Quarto Group.
The Old Brewery, 6 Blundell Street,
London N7 9BH, United Kingdom.
T (0)20 7700 6700 F (0)20 7700 8066
www.QuartoKnows.com

A catalogue record for this book is available from the British Library.

ISBN 978-07112-3842-8

Printed and bound in China

9 8 7 6 5

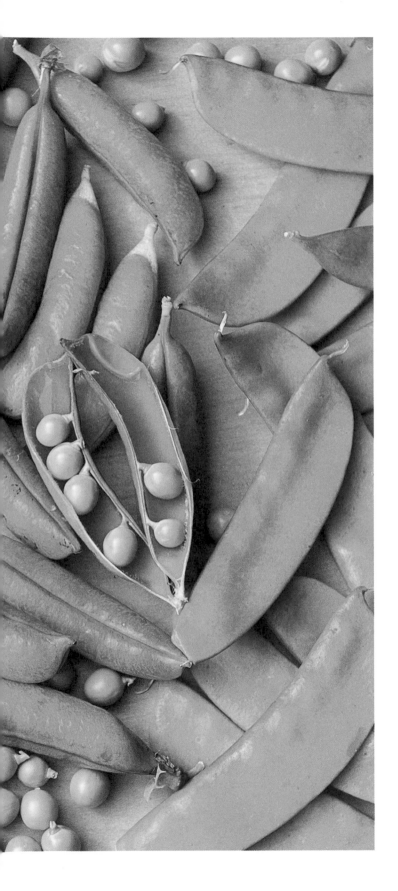

CONTENTS

30 PRACTICAL PROJECTS

1 **Broad bean support** 38

A pole-and-string structure to keep broad bean plants upright.

2 **Leafmould container** 42

Make the container and learn how to make perfect leafmould.

3 **Easy fruit cage** 46

A simple cage that can be reused, made from poles, jars, and netting.

4 **Simple cloches** 50

Two cloches that protect plants and stretch the growing season.

5 **Scarecrows** 54

Two easy-to-make scarecrows to help keep birds off your crops.

6 **Wooden planter** 60

Construct this versatile planter in any size to suit your space.

7 Raspberry wire support 64

A strong post-and-wire structure to support a row of raspberry canes.

8 Two-metre square bed 68

Grow a wide range of fruit and veg in this small raised bed.

9 Polytunnel hanging shelf 74

A hanging shelf to help raise pest-free seedlings and strawberries.

10 Basket planters 78

Create this rustic planter to fill with flowers or herbs.

11 Cherry tree frame 84

Tame an unruly cherry tree against this simple frame.

12 A-shaped bean frame 88

A really attractive wood and cane bean frame that's easy to make.

13 Timber raised beds 92

Make a large wooden raised bed and a small one for herbs.

14 Decorative obelisk 98

An elegant structure for climbing plants, such as beans and peas.

15 Boot tool 102

A neat design that helps to clean and remove dirty rubber boots.

16 Drying cabinet 106

Create your own drying system
to make some delicious treats.

17 Poly-cloche frame 112

Use this large frame for tender
crops and a longer growing season.

18 Seed trays & tools 118

Robust trays for raising seeds and
holding pots make a great gift set.

19 Slug-proof salad trays 124

Discover three ways to prevent
slugs from reaching salad crops.

20 Fitting out a shed 130

Transform your shed into a tidy
and efficient space for all your kit.

21 Hinged tool storage 136

Treble your tool storage space by
hanging an extra 'door' in a shed.

22 Covered hotbed 140

Make a hotbed for early peppers,
cucumbers, and aubergines.

23 Mini-greenhouse 146

A simple greenhouse for those
who don't have much space.

24 Cold frame 150

This frame has a copper base to
protect the contents from slugs.

25 Apple storage trays 154

A beautiful stacking set of trays to store your fruit harvests.

26 Carrot fly cover 160

This frame is fitted with fine mesh to keep insects away from crops.

27 Lean-to polyframe 166

Use the heat from a house wall to help grow tender vegetables.

28 Double compost bin 172

Make this indispensable strong, functional twin compost system.

29 Garden caddy 176

Keeps tools, gloves, and string close to hand while you work.

30 Growing bag cradle 182

Conceal a plastic growing bag in this beautiful timber table.

Using this book

The early pages show useful tools and materials, and some making tips. Most people will find a few helpful hints here, but if you are already a DIY expert, you could skip straight to the projects, although we would urge everyone to read the safety tips on p.17.

At the start of each project there is a symbol showing the 'difficulty level' and the number of hours you will need to complete it. ✚ A single blue dot in the difficulty rating bar means the project is easy enough for anyone to tackle. ✚✚✚✚✚ A 5 dot project may require a few more tools and a bit of wood-working experience. If you haven't made anything before, then start with something simple and work your way up.

In the 'hours to complete' bar, each blue dot equates to one hour. Timing is for the making stage, and it will vary, depending on your pace. Together with each project there are also gardening and usage tips.

Imperial measurement conversions are given to precise fractions in places where they are needed, or make sense for the project. In other situations measurements are rounded to the nearest unit. Hence, conversions aren't identical throughout the book.

INTRODUCTION

Gardeners start their fruit- and vegetable-growing journeys at different times and in different ways, but whatever your experience, there are always new things to learn.

Some people start their gardening journey by pushing a clove of garlic, or a bean, in the ground and then experiencing the thrill of watching green leaves grow. Some have a guiding hand from childhood and others start with herbs in pots, or scatter seed for salad leaves in a planter by the kitchen door. My love of gardening started with my grandfather. He grew terrific fruit and vegetables and was also a carpenter. I watched how he earthed up potatoes, planted tomatoes, or repaired a greenhouse door, and something settled inside me at a young age. What I learned was that we can all be resourceful, we can all solve problems and wherever we are on the gardening journey, there are always more things to learn and more ideas to follow.

This book comes from a passion for gardening combined with a passion for making things. It is also the result of my own particular skills matched with those of my husband Ben: I am a consummate 'build it fast to fulfil the task' maker and Ben is a perfectionist craftsman. I have been known to use a bread knife when lacking a saw and Ben can carve the most exquisite artworks. Together we have aimed to tackle some very specific and practical garden projects, each designed to help make the fruit and vegetable garden a more productive, efficient and attractive place. All these projects have been tried and tested and any shortcomings or revisions are mentioned in the text.

Over the following pages you will find ways to support climbing beans, and quick cheap options for making cloches or a fruit cage. You will also find some innovative ideas, like adding copper to a cold frame to keep out slugs, or making an elegant and effective covered hotbed.

There are also growing tips and suggestions for how to get the best out of the things you have made. But the biggest tip of all is to just go for it! This applies to planting that first clove of garlic, digging the soil, savouring a bountiful harvest, or making a few useful structures. The garden should be a fun place, so get making and growing and enjoy every single – and beautifully supported – bean.

I hope you enjoy making and using these projects as much as we did.

Joyce Russell

TOOLS & MATERIALS

Buying tools

You will need a basic tool kit for the projects in this book, but ensure you choose good quality products that will last.

If you are keen on making things for yourself, you may already have everything you require and possibly some additional tools that will help to speed things up a bit. But for those with no previous experience, make your selection from the tools shown here to build up a kit that suits your needs.

When shopping for tools you'll find a wide range of prices for the same tool, depending on the brand. Don't be tempted to buy the cheapest available. Very low prices often reflect substandard materials and design, and these tools are more likely to break with a small amount of stress and perform badly up to that point. At the other end of the spectrum, you will find comparatively expensive professional tools that will last a lifetime and are a joy to use. Between these two extremes there is a sensible middle-ground of good quality tools that won't break the bank.

A few more useful tools and extra equipment are discussed on pages 16–17.

Basic tool kit

Most of the projects in the book require just a few tools to complete, and each includes an individual list of what you will need. This guide shows you what each tool is used for.

Workbench: see Holding aids, page 17.

Tape measure: choose one 5m (16ft) long and strong enough for outdoor projects.

Hammer: a sturdy claw hammer allows you to knock nails in or to pull them out when required.

Heavy hammer: buy a long-handle sledgehammer for knocking posts into the ground and a smaller lump hammer for lighter work.

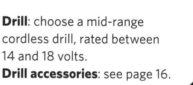

Drill: choose a mid-range cordless drill, rated between 14 and 18 volts.
Drill accessories: see page 16.

Handsaw: useful for cutting small pieces of timber; some can also be used as a square.

Screwdrivers: it is always useful to have a few different sizes to fit cross-head and slot-head screws.

Bradawl: makes guide holes for nails or screws.

Clamps: these have many uses – start with a pair of medium, 45cm (18in), and a pair of small, 15cm (6in) clamps. See also Holding aids, page 17.

Square: 15cm (6in) is a useful size, and you can hold a ruler next to it for wider timbers.

Bevel square: not essential, but useful for marking out diagonal cuts — use with a protractor for specific angles.

Straight-edge: 30cm (12in) steel rule and a straight, planed piece of timber for longer lines.

Jigsaw: a very versatile cutting tool for curved and straight cuts in timber and sheet material — buy different blades for coarse and fine cutting.

Hacksaw: these come in regular and junior sizes with replaceable hard steel blades for cutting through different materials.

Files and rasps: a file can also be used to flatten any nails or screws that accidently poke through timber. See also Sanding, rasping & planing, page 32.

Pliers: for cutting, pulling, and twisting wire.

Tin-snips: used to cut thin sheet metal.

Stanley knife: to cut thin sheet material and mark out crisp cutting lines on timber.

Block plane: a small plane for smoothing timber. See also Sanding, rasping & planing, page 32.

Staple gun: staples offer a fast and convenient way to fix polythene, netting or thin sheet material to timber – buy 6mm and 10mm staples.

Chisel: a 25mm (1in) is ideal — and hit it with a wooden mallet rather than a hammer.

Mitre box: an inexpensive device to guide a handsaw when making straight and angled cuts. See also Cutting & trimming, page 28.

Straight crowbar: 120cm (48in) is a good length for making holes in the ground for posts.

Spade, fork and shovel: for digging holes for posts and moving soil into raised beds.

Spirit level: it is useful to have two – 100cm (39in) or similar size for larger projects; 20cm (8in) for shorter lengths of timber.

Additional power tools

If you have the space and budget for two additional power tools, you will be able to work more accurately and efficiently.

Mitre (chop-saw)

A mitre saw, commonly known as a 'chop-saw', enables you to cut the ends of wooden components cleanly and at a perfect right angle, without the need to mark out the cuts with a square. The blade and motor swivel, which allow you to cut angles up to 45 degrees, and the more sophisticated saws that also tilt, enable you to cut compound angles.

Drill stands

The second tool we would recommend is a drill stand in which you can mount a power drill, then drill holes by pulling on a lever. This allows the depth, angle and entry point to be controlled more precisely. By setting up simple jigs, holes can be drilled quickly and accurately in multiple components without the need to mark the location of each hole individually.

Drill accessories

Cordless drills are wonderfully enabling tools that speed up screw-driving, bolt tightening, sanding, shaping, and, of course, drilling holes.

Ideally choose a drill that is supplied with two batteries so you won't have to stop work when one battery runs down. Buy an accessory kit that includes a range of drills, screwdriver bits and small sockets, which will allow you to make the most of your drill.

Using drill bits

Drill bits come in different patterns and have a few different uses:
- The most widely available pattern of drills are dual use, suitable for both wood and metal. Look out for sets that include a range of sizes from 1mm ($3/64$in) to 8mm ($5/16$in).
- Wood-boring bits have a fine pointed tip and 'spurs'. They make a tidier hole than a dual-purpose bit, but are only suitable for wood. A useful set of bits will range from 4mm ($5/32$in) to 12mm ($15/32$in)
- 'Spade' bits have a broad flat end, used to bore larger holes in timber. The holes they make are comparatively rough-edged, unless the bits are very sharp and used with care.

- Masonry bits have hardened tips that can make holes in concrete blocks and stone. They need a drill with a 'hammer action' setting to work properly.

Other accessories
- Screwdriver bits come in slot and cross-head patterns. Always use the right size and pattern for the screw in question (cross-head screws can be 'Pozidriv' [PZ] or 'Phillips' [PH]) and replace them when worn to avoid damaging the screw heads.
- A 'countersink' cuts a flared opening so that the screw head is neatly recessed, level with or below the surface of the timber.
- Combined drill and countersink bits speed up the process of drilling and countersinking if you have a lot of holes to drill.
- Depth stops are little collars that can be tightened onto the drill bit to limit the depth of the hole.

Holding aids

It is difficult to cut, shape, or drill accurately and safely unless the piece of wood or metal that you are working on is held securely and at a suitable height.

Workbench options

While it is possible to undertake these projects using chairs or the kitchen table for support, everything is easier and safer if you have some kind of workbench. A solid wooden bench with one or more vices is ideal, but few people have that luxury.

Small freestanding, folding benches are inexpensive and widely available. They have two top surfaces that clamp together to hold thin bits of timber or pipe, and pegs that can be inserted into holes in the surface, which are used for holding broader strips and irregular-shaped pieces.

If you have a small workshop or garden shed, consider buying or making a sturdy wooden bench. This can be much bigger, more stable and more robust than a lightweight freestanding bench. It can also house a good-sized vice, preferably built into the front, and it is a useful support on which to clamp and cut sheet material.

Choosing clamps

Whether you work on a solid wooden workbench or the kitchen table, it is important to have a few clamps. They come in a slightly bewildering array of shapes and sizes, but DIY enthusiasts will tell you that you can never have too many!

Start with two medium-sized F-pattern clamps with a capacity of, say, 45cm (18in). They don't have to be particularly heavy duty, unless you intend to use them for gluing jobs. Two lightweight 15cm (6in) F- or G-pattern clamps willl also be useful for securing smaller pieces.

Some clamps have a ratchet mechanism that tightens as you squeeze two handles together. These clamps are convenient because they can be operated with just one hand.

SAFETY TIPS

Tools have sharp edges and moving parts ready to injure you if you ignore basic safety precautions. In a careless moment you can cut yourself dangerously, sever a finger, or irreversibly damage an eye. Less obvious, but no less dangerous, is the noise power tools emit, which can lead to premature hearing loss if you do not wear ear protection. And working in a dusty environment without a safety mask can result in respiratory problems and dust-triggered allergies.

Buy safety glasses, ear protectors and disposable dust masks to protect you, and keep them close at hand so that using them becomes second nature, in the same way that you put on a seatbelt every time you drive.

Power tools come with specific safety advice; always read and follow it. Keep your hands well clear of cutting edges, and make sure that components are held securely while you are drilling or sawing.

However careful you are, accidents can happen, so keep a well-provisioned first-aid kit in your workspace, and plan how you will summon help and get appropriate attention in the event of a serious injury.

Choosing materials

Most materials for the projects in this book are easily available from DIY stores or online, but you can buy more specialist timbers, such as larch, from a sawmill. These guidelines will help you to choose materials appropriate to your needs.

Planed timber is a good choice for projects that will be handled frequently.

Timber

Garden woodwork is often left outside for most of the year, so durability is an important consideration. Some types of timber are naturally long-lasting; others will rot quickly unless treated with preservative. The more durable types are often worth the extra expense.

- **Durable timbers** include oak, chestnut, larch (European, not Japanese larch), western red cedar, Douglas fir and teak.
- **Non-durable timbers** include pine, spruce, ash and beech.
- **Rough-sawn timber** has a rustic, practical feel and is a good choice for larger projects.

Pressure treatment helps to protect non-durable timbers such as pine.

- **Planed timber** is more expensive than unplaned wood but, with no splinters, it is better for items that will be handled frequently. It is also available in a range of sizes, including small sections.
- **Pressure treatment** helps to protect cheaper, non-durable timbers from rotting. The treatment involves impregnating wood with a preservative liquid, and it is commonly used for softwood battens, planks, fence posts and decking. Check that the preservative used is suitable for garden equipment: 'Tanalith E', for example, is suitable for use in organic gardens if the timber has been allowed to dry for at least two weeks after treatment.

Hazel poles are a sustainable option, as they regrow from a central stump.

- **Decking boards** made from pressure-treated softwood are ideal for some of the projects in this book. These boards are readily available, reasonably durable and represent good value. Decking is usually machined with grooves on each side — deep on one side and shallow on the other — giving a choice of surface texture. Check that the preservative is garden-friendly before buying.
- **Hazel poles** harvested from 'coppiced' trees are the ultimate low-tech, sustainable material. Harvested from hedgerows (or plantations where they grow from previously cut stumps), they can be used with the bark intact or peeled. Hazel is not a durable material so don't expect a long life from the poles if they are left outside. If you live in the country you may be able to cut hazel poles yourself from hedgerows, but always ask the owners' permission first. Alternatively, specialist suppliers will deliver hazel (and other coppiced timber) in the small quantities used in these projects.

Wire, pipe, and copper

Strong galvanised wire and semi-rigid (alkathene) water pipe can be used for hoops in cloches and frames, and for other small structures. Both must be flexible enough to bend, but rigid enough to hold their shape.

- **3mm (1/8in) galvanised wire** is suitable for the fruit support projects. You can use thicker wire provided holes are large enough to accommodate it. Cut the wire with a hacksaw, stout pliers, or wire cutters.
- **25mm (1in) semi-rigid (alkathene) water pipe** can be used for many small projects. Cut water pipes with a hacksaw or pruning loppers.
- **Copper sheet material** is thin, flexible and slugs don't like to cross it. Use tin-snips to cut it and a hacksaw for cutting 19mm (3/4in) copper pipe.

Polythene sheet

Thick 600 to 800 gauge polythene, used to cover polytunnels, has high UV- and tear-resistance and can last ten years or more, but the thinnest building-grade polythene may last just one season. An affordable, strong medium thickness polythene is ideal for temporary coverings.

Wire or pipe can be used for the hoops in cloches and cold frames.

FIXINGS AND FINISHES

FIXINGS: Choose from these fixings for long-lasting results:
- **Stainless steel screws** will not rust and are worth the extra cost. They look good, are very long-lasting and will not break if you wish to dismantle a project.
- **Decking screws** are heavy-duty external grade fixings used to secure decking to a substructure. They are also slow to rust.
- **Galvanised nails** will not rust and therefore do not make rust stains on timber. 'Oval' nails have a small head that can be discreetly punched below the surface. Clout nails have a broad flat head.
- **Panel pins** are skinny nails with a very small head and a shaft 1.5mm (1/16in) in diameter.
- **Galvanised drive screws** have a domed head and a spiral fluted shaft. Sometimes called 'zinc nails', they are commonly used to fix corrugated iron, but are useful for larger garden projects too.
- **Combined screw and plug fixings** are used to fix timber to masonry. They are easy to use and ideal for securely mounting timber to block or concrete walls.
- **Plated steel screws** look good initially but soon rust outdoors, so are best avoided.

FINISHES: Your choice of wood finish is partly down to personal preference, but always check its suitability for use near fruit and vegetable crops.
- **Preservative wood stains** enhance the appearance and increase the weather resistance of non-durable timbers.
- **Oils** are easy to apply, but offer comparatively short-lived clear finishes. Some, such as teak oil, combine a preservative with a gentle stain.
- **Paint** in solid colours suitable for outdoor use can add drama.
- **Nude** timbers left with no treatment at all will bleach in rain and sunlight, fading to a pleasing grey colour. Durable timbers are the best types to leave untreated.

This range of screws, nails, panel pins and fixings will be suitable for most garden DIY projects.

MAKING
TIPS

7 reasons to make your own

This book presents a wide range of beautiful and practical garden structures to make. Most are cheaper than shop-bought, but there are plenty of other reasons to make your own.

1 You can't always buy what you want
Sometimes it is better to design and make your own solution to a problem than to settle for a bought option that doesn't quite do what you want. For example, this boot cleaner was designed to make cleaning boots easier and to pull them off too.

2 It's easy to make the right size
It can be difficult to find a planter for a narrow window ledge, or a cold frame that fits exactly into the corner by the shed. The projects in this book can be scaled up or down to fit the space you have. Simply alter the dimensions accordingly.

3 You can improve what you grow
Think plant protection here, without the need to invest in expensive structures. Or frames for fruit, good compost bins, and supports for beans that won't fall over. These pages are full of great ideas to help you get the best from your fruit and vegetable garden.

4 You don't need to hire a carpenter
The projects in this book are designed to be easy for an amateur to make. So if you want to create more tool storage by fitting an extra folding door in the shed, then have a go. It can be liberating to discover what is possible without calling in professional help.

5 Handmade can be more beautiful
This is all a matter of opinion, of course, but when making your own, you do get to choose the materials, colours, and finishes to suit your garden. There are no fixed rules; you can add or take away from these designs, or change them altogether if you want.

6 You can make a perfect gift
Handmade items have that personal touch and make wonderful gifts for friends and family. Why not make this useful caddy, or a planter filled with seasonal flowers? Or try your hand at a bean frame or a compost bin to delight any practical gardener.

7 It's fun for all the family
You can get the whole family involved in these creative projects. Children love sanding and hammering and are there to help when it's time to pick your crops. It's amazing how quickly a budding carpenter can become a budding gardener too.

Getting started

There are lots of projects to choose from in this book, so how do you decide what's right for you? These tips will help you to make your selection.

The perfect size →

Consider the dimensions of the project and make sure it is right for you. Some will fit into any garden, but you may need to tweak others to suit a small space.

• It is easy to scale some dimensions up or down to make a shorter or wider raised bed, or shelf for your polytunnel, for example. Measure carefully and draw out the new sizes if changing any measurements.

• 'Measure twice, cut once!' This is a good mantra to keep in mind, and don't cut until you are sure of the exact sizes you need.

LEFT Lay out all your tools and materials before you start.

← Choosing a project

If you have never made anything before, start with something simple and work your way up to more complex projects — the difficulty ratings offer a guide.

• Take a look at what you need and read through all the 'making' steps so you have a rough idea of what you are aiming to create.

• Decide where the project will go, or if the person for whom you are making it has sufficient space.

• Make decisions about finishes, such as paint colour, at a later stage, if you prefer to work that way.

← Assemble what you need

Look at the list of tools and materials for the project that you want to make.

• Assemble all the materials and lay them out so you know where the next piece is when you need it.

• Keep tools in familiar places so you don't have to hunt through the garage or shed every time you need your hammer or drill bit.

• Make a safe and clear workspace. Remove potential hazards, such as garden tools, that might fall over, trip you up, or make working difficult.

Marking out straight lines

Ensure you make neat and accurate cuts by marking
out your lines carefully first. Use the correct tools
and a sharp pencil and you shouldn't go wrong.

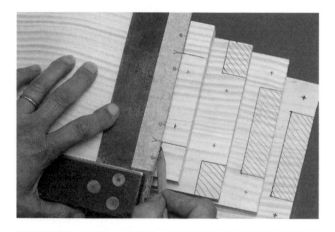

Creating diagonal cuts →

Mark these out using a bevel square, or make a paper
template as a quick and simple guide.

• A bevel square has an adjustable section that you
  can set at an angle. Set with a protractor if you want
  a specific angle.
• Alternatively, try folding a piece of paper or card to
  give the required angle. Make sure the paper doesn't
  wrinkle or move when running a pencil along the
  edge of this marking guide.

← Using a square

This tool enables you to draw consistent straight lines
at right angles to the edge of the timber.

• Use the square to mark down the edge, as well as the
  face of the timber, when marking a cutting line across
  a piece of wood. Follow the lines when cutting, to
  ensure a straight horizontal and vertical cut.
• A quick way to mark the same points on several pieces
  of timber is to stick masking tape on the blade of the
  square. Mark measuring points on the tape and use
  them to mark the lines of straight cut-outs (as shown).

← Marking longer lines

For some pieces you may need to use a 'straight-edge'
to mark long lines.

• A 100cm (36in) steel rule is a useful tool for marking
  straight lines. The hard edge will also not wear down
  or become distorted with frequent use.
• Measure and mark two or more points and lay the
  rule between these to draw a straight line.
• Alternatively, use a length of wood, or a piece of cut
  plywood, as a straight-edge, provided the edge *is*
  perfectly straight and isn't bowed. However, you may
  find wood loses its straight edge after frequent use.

Drawing curves & shapes

Marking out complex shapes and curves requires a little more skill but card or paper templates and adaptable nail-and-string compasses can help.

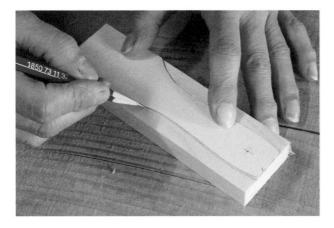

Marking a curve →
An even curved edge can make all the difference to the look of a well-crafted piece.
• Tie one end of a piece of string to a fixed pin or nail, and tie a pencil to the other end. Use this to draw an even curve as shown. Keep the string taut and maintain a smooth action while drawing.
• Shorten or lengthen the string to draw a tighter or wider curve. Practise on a piece of paper before marking the wood.

← Drawing unusual shapes
You will get the most consistent results by drawing out the pattern you require before starting to cut.
• Draw straight onto the timber only if you are confident. It is usually better to make a paper or cardboard template first and to draw around this.
• For symmetrical patterns fold the paper in half, draw half the design, cut it out, and open out.
• You will not need a template if you are artistic and prefer a freehand look.

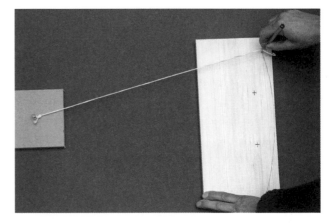

← Creating slots and handles
Make these comfortable to use and large enough to suit the size of your hand.
• Mark out a drilling point at each end of the handle slot. Make the distance between the points slightly wider than your hand.
• A large drill hole will automatically mark the end curve of the slot. Draw a line across the top and bottom to define the rest of the cut.
• Marking waste areas with a series of parallel lines, known as crosshatching, makes it easier to see the bits you want to remove, and prevents mistakes.

Cutting & trimming

Clean, accurate cuts can help projects run more smoothly. A sharp saw, clamps and a mitre box are among the essential tools you will need.

← Using a mitre box

A mitre box is a simple and inexpensive cutting guide that enables you to make precise cuts with a handsaw.

- Choose a mitre box with both right angle and diagonal slots.
- Hold the mitre box in a vice, or clamp it to a worktop to ensure it doesn't slip when in use.
- Run a handsaw through the guide slots to make accurate square cuts across small pieces of timber.
- A sharp saw will cut the timber more accurately and give a smoother finish.

← Trimming excess

Trimming small pieces of excess timber can make all the difference to the look of a finished project. Carefully trim unintentional overlaps when the article has been assembled.

- It is sometimes easier to cut off surplus timber when it is fixed into position, rather than trying to work out the cutting angles accurately beforehand.
- Hold the timber, or assembled piece, firmly so hands are safe and the piece can't move while you are sawing.

The versatile jigsaw →

A jigsaw will cut in any direction, across the grain or with it, and is ideal for cutting shapes from planks of wood or from sheet material such as plywood.

• Always secure small pieces with a clamp.
• Hold the jigsaw with two hands and only switch it on and off when it is firmly pressed against the surface of the timber.
• To cut out a shape from the middle of a piece of timber, drill a hole large enough to fit the blade through in the section of wood that you plan to remove.

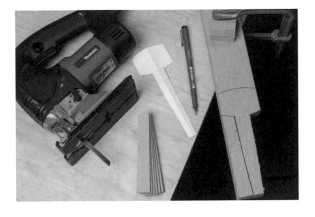

← Cutting multiple components

It is sometimes possible to cut several identical pieces at once, which will speed up the making process.

• Use a clamp to hold duplicate pieces on top of one another and cut carefully through all the layers. Make sure all pieces are lined up accurately and that there is no room for movement before starting to cut.
• Line up small duplicate pieces. Clamp them tightly and cut through them all with a sharp saw.

Check the width of the cut →

Saw blades cut out a significant slot (known as a 'kerf' to a woodworker) and you should allow for this when marking out components.

• Remember that a saw cut is far wider than a pencil line.
• A jigsaw or handsaw can take out a 1-2mm ($3/64$in – $5/64$in) kerf, depending on the blade.
• A chop-saw kerf can be as much as 4mm ($5/32$in).
• Cut on the waste side of the marked line, rather than through the middle of it.

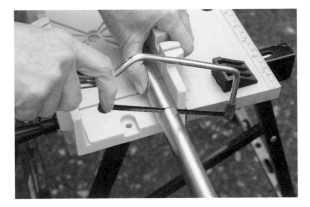

← Cutting metal and plastic pipe

You will need a hacksaw to cut through metal parts and to make neat cuts through plastic or alkathene water pipe.

• Securely clamp the piece that you want to saw.
• Practice a steady, straight sawing action: hacksaw blades are thin and will bend or snap if too much sideways pressure is applied.
• The friction of cutting through metal generates heat. Don't touch the cut end until it has cooled down and remember to file any rough sawn edges before using.

Making drilling holes

Follow these tricks of the trade to make accurate drilling holes and recess screw heads flush with the timber surface for a neat finish.

GENERAL DRILLING TIPS

- **Timber can split** if nails or screws are fixed too close to a cut end. Drill holes first to avoid this problem.
- **Apply steady pressure** so the drill bit bites through the timber. Ease back on speed and pressure, or support the back with a piece of scrap timber, if a clean exit hole is required.
- **Make a dent** with a nail or bradawl first if drilling into a hard material. This helps to prevent the end of the bit skidding before it finds purchase.

↓ Pilot and clearance holes

These two types of hole are often used when fixing two pieces of timber together.

- Pilot holes are drilled to help lead the point of a screw into the timber. They should be smaller than the diameter of screw you intend to use, so the thread bites.
- Clearance holes are drilled through the top piece of timber, so the screw shaft slides through them before fixing into the timber below. Make these holes roughly the same diameter as the screw shaft and smaller than the head.

← Marking multiple components

This is a fast and accurate technique for marking multiple, identical, drilling holes.

- Fold a piece of card so that it sits precisely over the edge of the timber to the required measurement (as shown). Mark drilling points on one edge of the card. Use this guide to mark multiple pieces with a pencil or bradawl.
- When marking sawn ends, fold the card to cover the end. Then mark drilling points, and punch through the holes with a sharp pencil to mark the wood underneath.

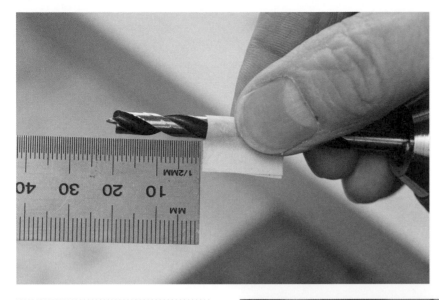

← Fixed depth holes

Some drill bit sets also contain collars, which fit round the shaft of the bit to set a fixed drilling depth. If there are no collars in your set, try these simple alternatives.

- Fit a piece of masking tape round the bit at the required height. Keep a close eye and stop drilling when the edge of the tape touches the drilled surface.
- Use a black marker to draw a line on the bit. This is more difficult to see than tape.

Using a countersink →

Use a countersink bit to make a depression, so screw heads sit flush with the timber surface.

- Screw heads can push into the surface of soft woods, but the timber may split. A countersink bit makes a much neater job of recessing the heads.
- Don't cut too deeply and aim for the same depth on all holes for a consistent finish.
- You can buy countersink bits for an electric drill or hand-held tools for this job.

← Larger holes

Sometimes you may want to use a spade bit to make a hole with a large diameter, or a longer bit to make a deeper hole.

- Spade bits come in a range of sizes and will cut a hole of a fixed diameter. When drilling, support the back of the wood with a scrap of timber to prevent splitting.
- Buy a bit that is long enough to drill through a large section of wood. And don't try to make two shorter holes meet up.

Sanding, rasping & planing

The tools for these jobs create smooth surfaces that are comfortable to handle and free from splinters. These tips will ensure you achieve the best results.

← Using abrasive sanding sheets

Sanding sheets (sandpaper) are used to remove any splinters and rough edges that would make materials uncomfortable to handle.

- Abrasives can be very coarse, very fine or somewhere in between. Fine grades remove very little material but create a smooth surface; coarse grades will remove much more, but leave a scratched surface.
- Wrap abrasives around a wooden or cork backing block: this will apply an even pressure and makes sanding a flat surface much easier.

Files and rasps →

Metal files and wood rasps are both useful woodworking tools.

- Files are suitable for smoothing metal or wood. Use a two-handed technique and keep the file as flat as possible when moving it across the surface.
- Use a rasp on the edges of particularly rough-sawn timber where you need to remove large splinters. It is worth practising your technique to ensure an even finish without taking out too much material.

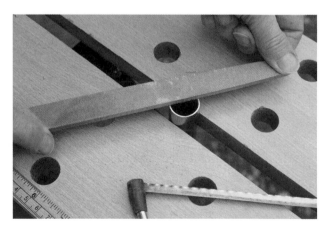

← Planing timber

A plane is used to smooth rough timber and to put an even chamfer or bevel along an edge.

- A block plane is small enough to hold in one hand and ideal for small pieces of wood. Use a smooth motion to take off an even curl of timber.
- A smoothing plane is larger and requires two hands. When using this plane hold the timber securely by clamping it or putting it in a vice.
- Plane blades must be kept sharp to slice off curls smoothly, without snagging the wood.

Lining up & levelling

Even surfaces and aligned timbers will ensure your structures function properly and look smart, so take time to check levels and spacings carefully.

← Using a spirit level

There are long levels, short levels, and little ones that you can hang on a length of taut string. A short level, which can be held in one hand, is probably the most versatile type and a good buy for beginners.

- Check the spirit level in all relevant directions: a fence post may look straight when viewed from the front, but still lean forward or back.
- You may need supports to keep everything aligned until the relevant components are fixed in place.

← Making a spacer

Use small pieces of wood as spacers to inset and line up boards to a fixed measurement to create even gaps.

- Gaps can be included in joints where components meet, and between slats. Gaps help to shed water and allow ventilation.
- Cut a piece of scrap timber to the width of the gap required and long enough to line up with the relevant pieces. You may need several spacers for gaps between slats. Remove when timbers are in place.

← Eyeball it!

It is sometimes more important to stand back and check how something actually looks than to get too hung up with straight lines and levels.

- Look along the structure from one end. Do some parts seem higher than you want, or does one corner dip down? If so, you can tweak things a little until they all look straight.
- You may have to compromise on sloping ground; aim for what looks right and functions well.

Assembling structures

Putting together simple or complex structures accurately is not always easy, but follow these expert tips carefully and you won't go wrong.

Providing support →

Make sure that structures are supported when components are hammered into place: the force of a blow can knock unsupported joints apart.

• Try to assemble wooden features on a flat hard surface. Turn the structure so you are hammering downwards and the hard surface resists the force.

• Hold the head of a sledgehammer against the back of a post if it is already in the ground and you are fixing on boards. Without such support, the post will move.

← Putting together frames

Several projects in the book are based on frames. Some are simply four pieces of wood screwed together, but whatever the size, proportions, or number of components, it is important that frames are level, square and straight.

• Measure corner to corner, to ensure that the two diagonals are equal, or check that all corners are at right angles before final fixing takes place.

• Lay out all pieces and check how they fit together, and ensure the frame lies flat when assembled.

← Don't rush

Your project may be in place for many years so don't rush the assembly stage.

• If glue or concrete are the best options, then use them. Finish the project the next day, if necessary, so these have time to set.

• Use clamps if you need to hold parts together when fixing. They prevent parts from moving and ensure a precise, tight fit.

• Correct mistakes at an early stage, rather than notice them every time you use the item.

30 PRACTICAL PROJECTS

Broad bean support

Keep your broad beans
upright with a pole
and string support.
This simple structure
prevents plants blowing
over and keeps the row
tidy and contained.
It also makes flowers
accessible to bees and
pods easy to find.

You will need

**For a bean row
180cm (72in) in length**

- **Poles or narrow posts**
  8 x 170cm long, 40mm
  diameter (66in, 1¹/₂in) or longer
  if you grow tall varieties
- **Strong string**

TOOLS
- Straight crowbar
- Heavy hammer
- Scissors

Bean rows should make a small footprint on the soil, but they don't always
do what we think they should. Plants can end up sprawled on the ground
with blossoms squashed and beans eaten by slugs. To prevent this, it
makes sense to build a supportive frame for the row rather than provide
a cane for each individual plant. A few poles, stout canes, or 25mm (1in)
square timbers will support a fence of strings, and you can start with two
sets of horizontal strings and add more as the beans grow taller.

    Some broad bean varieties can grow very tall and it's not unusual for
spring-planted types to achieve 2m (6ft 6in) in good growing conditions,
so ensure your frame meets their requirements or nip out the growing
points to keep plants within the one you've made. Over-wintered varieties
don't usually grow quite as tall, but they can easily reach 1.2m (4ft).

Sturdy supports will help to
guarantee a good crop of beans.

Making the broad bean support

STEP 1 CUT THE POLES

You can start plants under a cloche early in the year. Remove the covering when beans are around 23cm (9in) tall and starting to need some support. Make sure all sides of the row are clear and weed-free before putting the frame in place. Cut your poles to length.

STEP 2 PUT POLES IN PLACE

Make holes with the crowbar: two at each end of the row and one every 60cm (24in) along each side of the row. For a 180cm (72in) row this means eight holes. Put a pole in each hole and knock them all in with the heavy hammer to a depth of about 45cm (18in).

STEP 3 LOOP STRING AROUND POLES

Tie one end of the string to one pole at the end of a row, 15cm (6in) above the ground. Walk along each side of the row, looping the string around each pole, so that it encircles the beans. Maintain an even height and tie the string to the pole you started with.

STEP 4 BUILD LAYERS AS PLANTS GROW

Add more layers of string as the plants grow. Position each layer roughly 15cm (6in) apart; you don't have to be very precise as long as plants are adequately supported. For extra support, if needed, you can also tie pieces of string horizontally across the rows in between the poles.

STEP 5 TUCK STEMS IN

You may need to tuck plants back inside the strings if they attempt to grow out sideways. Take great care not to snap the stems or to knock flowers from plants. Wandering stems can always miss a few strings lower down and be tucked back in at a higher level.

STEP 6 ALLOW FOR EXTRA GROWTH

A healthy row of plants may start to push the strings out a little. You can always add in extra canes or sticks at any point if needed. If a row outgrows the height of the frame, you can either nip out the growing points, or use more canes to extend the frame's height.

SOWING AND GROWING TIPS FOR BROAD BEANS

Broad beans aren't fussy plants and they will grow in all sorts of soils. These tips will help you to grow the best crop and the frame will keep plants in line.

Broad bean flowers are self-fertile but bees will help to boost crops.

- **Choose the right variety** of broad bean for the time of year you plan to sow them. 'Aquadulce Claudia' is good for mid- to late autumn sowings, and 'Imperial Green Longpod' and 'Jubilee Hysor' are two of our favourite spring-sown varieties.
- **Dig out** a 25cm (10in) deep trench and fill the bottom two-thirds with garden compost, then top up the remaining third with soil to bring it level with the surface. Use coarse, or partially broken down compost, which will help to retain moisture in the trench as well as provide nutrients.
- **Sow beans** 5cm (2in) deep and 20cm (8in) apart, in double rows 20cm (8in) apart. Allow 90cm (36in) between each set of double rows. Plants require plenty of light and air and you will also need space to walk easily through the rows to pick them.
- **Put a few extra seeds** at the end of the row, or in pots; you can then transplant these to fill any gaps.
- **Protect young plants** from slugs and snails and if these pests are a persistent problem, try starting plants in pots where they cannot reach your seedlings. Then plant out only when the seedlings reach 15cm (6in) in height.
- **Cover** autumn, late winter, and early spring sowings with a cloche to give plants a head start.
- **Keep soil watered**, especially when plants are in flower.
- **Flowers** are self-fertile, but you will get a much better set of pods if bees have good accesss to the flowers to pollinate them, so remove any coverings when plants start to bloom.
- **Harvest** when the beans have swollen to a good size in the pods, but before they become starchy. For many varieties, the beans lose their flavour as their green colour fades.

Pick pods when beans are young and tender.

Grow a few extra plants to fill gaps in rows.

Leafmould container

This useful container takes just two hours to make. You then fill it with leaves and wait a year for the leafmould to form, which you can use to improve soil, make potting mixes, or help seeds to germinate.

If you poke down to take a look at the lower layers of a forest floor you will find a dark crumbly mix that slides between the fingers like silk. This is leafmould at its best. It doesn't take much effort for the gardener to mimic the beautiful sustainable cycle of the forest to create this wonderful resource, but do make it from your own leaves, rather than raiding woods.

All you need is a supply of leaves and a simple frame to put them in. The structure only has to hold the leaves in place; the top stays open to the air and rain, which promotes the micro-organisms that slowly break them down. This container solves the 'what to do with all the fallen leaves' problem and it is strong enough to last for a decade or more, while turning leaves into a magical mix for the garden.

You will need

For an 80cm x 80cm x 92cm (32in x 32in x 36in) leafmould container

- **Timber**
  4 x 150cm long, 80mm diameter (60in, 3in) fence posts
- **Fencing wire**
  92cm x 330cm x 2.5cm (36in x 150in x 1in) mesh size, galvanised
- **Fencing staples**
  2cm (³⁄₄in) long, galvanised

TOOLS
- Straight crowbar
- Sledgehammer
- Hammer
- Tape measure
- Wire cutters

Enjoy the bounty of glorious autumn leaves and make use of this free resource.

Making the leafmould container

Clear enough space so you won't trample plants or get scratched by branches when making the container. A level site is ideal, but this project is so simple that you can also put it on a slope or an uneven base. Any corner of the garden will do.

Use a crowbar to make holes and stand the posts in them. A rough initial placing will help you choose the right size for your container, but precision is less important than locating a spot where the posts won't hit stones when knocked in. The sides don't have to be square.

Use a sledgehammer to knock the posts into the ground. Aim to keep the posts vertical and don't let them lean in so that they reduce the bin size. Knock the posts down until they are firmly in the ground, even if this means they end up at different heights.

Line up the edge of the netting against the front right-hand post and use staples to hold it in place. Unroll the netting around the posts. It is useful to have an extra pair of hands at this stage: one person to stretch the netting while the other hammers in staples.

The netting should reach around all four sides and back to the front right-hand post. Try not to hammer staples in all the way when fixing the final edge against the post, as you will need to remove them next year when you open the bin to take out the leafmould.

Loose leaves will settle down to a lower level over time. If you want to speed up this process, or you have more leaves than the container initially seems to hold, you can push the leaves down, or help a small child to jump around on top!

TIPS FOR MAKING AND USING LEAFMOULD

Leafmould will add precious humus to any impoverished soil and it also helps improve water retention in light sandy soils.

Maple leaves break down quickly.

- **Leaf fall** can last for several weeks. Some trees lose their leaves early in the autmnn, while others lose theirs later, so keep adding leaves to the container until all the leaves have fallen.
- **Don't cover** a leafmould bin; a certain amount of moisture is needed for the leaves to break down. And there is no need to turn the contents, because everything will eventually rot down. In fact, there is no need to do anything other than trim the area around the bin so weeds don't grow through and seed into the contents.
- **All leaves rot slowly**, but oak, chestnut and plane take longer; maple, hazel and ash break down relatively quickly. A year is probably the minimum time to convert fibrous leaves into a fine crumbly mix.
- **Open the front** of the container after one year. Remove any loose debris from the top of the settled contents and shovel the rest into bags. The leafmould will continue to break down in the bags until you are ready to use it. You can then refill the bin with more leaves.
- **Leafmould** is a good substitute for peat in homemade potting mixes. It adds 'humus', which is a sticky substance that holds onto nutrients and water, and then releases them slowly into the soil.
- **Scatter a layer** of leafmould in the bottom of seed drills to improve germination. It provides a fine, moisture-retaining medium which is perfect for young carrots.
- **Chard and spinach** do particularly well if a mulch of leafmould is scattered around growing plants.
- **Leafmould can help** lower soil pH (increase acidity) and it contains useful amounts of calcium, magnesium, phosphorous and potassium.

Store leafmould in bags after one year, ready to use on the garden.

Leafmould is the perfect mulch for many crops, such as spinach and chard (above).

EXPERT TIP

Create larger nets by sewing together narrower lengths using a sewing machine and strong, rot-proof thread.

Easy fruit cage

DIFFICULTY LEVEL ⊕⊕⊕⊕⊕⊕⊕⊕⊕⊕

HOURS TO COMPLETE 🕐🕐🕐🕐🕐🕐🕐🕐🕐🕐

3

Cover bushes with an easy-to-assemble fruit cage to prevent birds from stealing your crops. This will protect a large or small area and the height is easy to adjust to suit any size of gardener.

Bush fruits, such as raspberries, currants and gooseberries, are some of the most rewarding and tasty crops to grow in the garden. Unfortunately, birds seem to like them as much as we do and, if you are unlucky, they can strip all the ripe berries from bushes before you get a chance to harvest them.

You can buy a fruit cage of course, but these are often expensive frames covered with wire or netting, and most are permanent structures. It is much easier and cheaper to make the one shown here, and you can reuse this simple pole-and-net system for many years. Put the cage up in late spring to keep bullfinches off the blossom, and take it down when the last bushes have finished fruiting. For the rest of the year, it makes sense to leave bushes uncovered so that insect-eating birds can scratch underneath and dispatch pests, and their eggs and larvae.

You will need

For a bed measuring 370cm x 370cm x 180cm (144in x 144in x 72in)

- **Poles or narrow posts**
  16 x 250cm long and 40mm in diameter (96in x 1¹/₂in) or 40mm (1¹/₂in) square
- **Post covers**
  16 empty jam jars, or plastic drinks bottles
- **Weights**
  Bricks, stones, or lengths of timber
- **Netting**
  800cm x 800cm (324in x 324in) strong and woven if possible

TOOLS
- Straight crowbar
- Loppers or saw
- Small heavy hammer
- Two long poles or long-handled brushes

Making the easy fruit cage

Use a crowbar to make holes 60cm (24in) deep. Space 12 holes evenly around the bed and four in the middle. Spacing doesn't have to be precise; if you can't get the crowbar in the ground at one point, then try another a little further away.

Put the poles into the holes and knock them down with the hammer to leave 180cm (72in) above the ground. Again, this length does not have to be precise, but it is a good idea to leave some headroom to make it easy to work in the fruit cage.

Invert an empty jam jar, or plastic drinks bottle, over the end of each pole. Take care with glass jars and keep them away from children. Plastic bottles are more noticeable but they are unlikely to break. Netting will slide freely over the bottles.

USING YOUR EASY FRUIT CAGE

Birds will hop around the edge of the netting looking for a way in, so ensure you do not to leave any gaps where they could enter.

Redcurrants and other fruit tempt birds when left unprotected.

- **Remove weights** and lift the netting at any point to get inside the cage. Throw the netting up onto the top of the cage when picking and when you have finished weigh it down again.
- **Dismantle the cage** and put it away when the bushes have finished cropping. Stuff the netting into a sack and tie the top so you can hang it up in a shed. Leave the poles in place, but remember that untreated timber will only last a couple of years.
- **Currants, gooseberries, raspberries** and many hybrid fruits will all grow well inside the cage. Prune bushes each winter so they don't grow taller than the net.
- **Strip off the netting** and let the birds clear up any fallen, burst or straggler berries when the main harvest is finished. Birds will also pick off some pests that are on the plants or in the soil around the roots.
- **Fruit bushes** that are hidden in corners near the house may escape attack from birds for a few years, but a large block of bushes makes an easy target and the berries will need to be covered in a cage like this.
- **Use the same system** to make shorter covers for crops like brassicas. It also works well as a 40cm (16in) tall structure to go over a newly planted onion bed; birds will pull out onion sets by their dry brown necks at any opportunity. Remove the cover once green shoots grow up.

STEP 4 LAY THE NETTING ON THE GROUND

Stretch the netting out on the ground along one side of the fruit bed. Position so that it allows roughly the right amount of overlap at each end. Ease out any twists and tangles at this stage so the netting moves freely when stretched over the bed.

STEP 5 LIFT THE NETTING OVER THE BED

Ask someone to help at this stage, if possible. Use long poles to lift the front edge of the netting above the height of the bushes. Walk along either side of the bed until the netting covers the cage without snagging on bushes or damaging blossom.

STEP 6 WEIGH DOWN THE EDGES

Pull the netting into position, leaving 30cm (12in) overlap on the ground along all four sides. Place weights along one side of the netting to hold it down. Stretch the net tight and do the same on the opposite side, and then on the remaining two sides.

Lift one side to enter the cage and harvest fruit.

A bed about 3.7m (12ft) square is large enough for a wide range of fruits.

Simple cloches

You will need

For a cloche 210cm (84in) in length

- **Clear polythene**
  365cm x 152cm (144in x 60in)
- **Galvanised wire or pipe**
  5 x 122cm (48in) bendable, semi-rigid
- **Rot-proof string**
- **Sticks**
  2 x sticks, roughly 38cm (15in) in length
- **Stones, bricks or similar**

TOOLS

- Hacksaw
- Scissors

Revolutionise your vegetable growing with this simple cloche. One of the easiest projects to make, it is also one of the most useful, providing cold-weather protection for young and vulnerable plants.

You can extend the growing season at both ends of the year with a few cloches. They shield plants from frost, wind and heavy rain, creating a sheltered environment where young plants can flourish, and many early spring sowings will get off to a good start given a few weeks under this type of insulating cover. In addition, a cloche can help to protect crops against flying pests and some airborne diseases.

It is also possible to harvest crops, such as winter salad, spinach and oriental greens, through the colder months with the aid of this simple polythene structure. A cloche can also be used to get an early start to the gardening year by sowing peas, beans, kohlrabi, beetroot, early carrots, early potatoes, radishes and any salad leaves under it in late winter.

Use this cloche system to fit any length of crop row: simply adjust the number of hoops and the length of cover accordingly. You can also swap the polythene for rain-permeable crop cover, which allows water through.

Rows of peas and broad beans get off to an early start.

Making a simple cloche

STEP 1 CUT HOOPS TO LENGTH

Cut the wire to length and bend it to form five even, equal hoops. If using semi-rigid pipe, this will only stay in a hoop shape when pushed into the ground (Step 2). On exposed sites, use six hoops per cloche to make a stronger structure.

STEP 2 SET UP THE HOOPS

Push hoops firmly into the ground, 50cm (20in) apart, and to the same height. Push the sticks in at each end of the row, tie the string to one stick and then unroll it to the top of the first hoop. Wind the string once around the top of the hoop.

STEP 3 MAKE A STRING 'TOP RIDGE'

Keep the string taut and move along the row winding it around the top of the hoops. Tie the string to the stick at the opposite end of the row. This will give you a tight straight ridge of string along the top of the frame.

STEP 4 BURY ONE POLYTHENE EDGE

Spread the polythene over the frame, allowing some extra material on either side. Also make sure there is enough polythene to close each end. Pile soil over one side of polythene to weigh it down; this edge will remain weighted when the cloche is opened.

STEP 5 WEIGH DOWN THE OTHER EDGE

Use bricks, tiles, or timber to weigh down the other side of the polythene. Use weights that will keep the polythene in place in windy conditions, but are easy to remove when the cloche is opened. Make sure no sharp edges will rip the cover.

STEP 6 CLOSE THE ENDS

Gather the polythene around the stick at one end of the cloche. Keep the stick outside the polythene so the top doesn't make any rips in the covering. Secure the ends with a large stone, brick, or equivalent, and repeat at the other end.

Creating a rigid cloche

This rigid cloche has open ends, so it will not hold heat as well as a closed one. However, it does provide good protection for plants without having to monitor ventilation. Use clear, corrugated sheet material and wire hoops.

STEP 1 POSITION THE FIRST HOOPS

Cut wire lengths to the width of the sheet material, plus 60cm (24in). This allows 30cm (12in) to push into the soil on each side. Push a hoop into the ground at each end and space others roughly 90cm (36in) apart in between. Sow or plant your crops.

STEP 2 FIT THE COVER

After planting, bend the sheet material over the hoops until it just touches them and the ground along each side. Start at the midpoint and fit a second set of hoops over the top of the sheet material, so the plastic is secured between two hoops.

SOWING AND GROWING TIPS FOR A SIMPLE CLOCHE

Prepare the ground in autumn and sow peas and broad beans under cloches if you want the earliest crop of pods.

Enjoy an early crop of salad leaves by sowing them under a cloche in late winter.

- **Prepare the ground** by digging in compost, or making a trench, before putting the cloche in place. Peas and beans appreciate a scattering of lime if the soil is too acidic (low pH).
- **Put cloches up** a week before sowing to give the ground a chance to warm up underneath.
- **Try sowing** 'Meteor', 'First Early May', or other winter hardy varieties of peas under a cloche in mid-autumn. These will often provide the earliest spring crops.
- **Slugs** can hide under polythene edges, so use organic-approved controls underneath the cloche when seedlings are due to emerge.
- **Ventilation** is important and temperatures rise quickly in a small sealed space. Open each end of a closed cloche, or throw the covering back completely if the weather starts to warm up. Remember to close the covers again on cold and frosty nights.
- **Soil will dry out** under a cloche with an impermeable covering. Open the cover and water as necessary to ensure good germination and to keep the soil damp round the roots of small seedlings. You can water over the top of water-permeable coverings.
- **Harden plants off** as they start to outgrow the cloche. To do this, simply open the covers during the day and then cover your plants again at night, leaving just the ends open. Keep young plants covered if possible until really low temperatures and frosty conditions have passed.
- **Put cloches away** in a shed when not in use. Bring them out again when needed and they should give many years of service before you need to replace the covers.

Throw back the cover on hot days.

Remove the cloche when plants reach the polythene.

Scarecrows

Scarecrows are fun to make and raise a smile whenever they are spotted in a garden. Children love to help create these exciting new additions to the vegetable patch, and a scarecrow really can help keep birds off the brassicas.

Most birds are a pleasure to have in the garden, but there are some that do serious damage to crops. Pigeons can strip the leaves off newly planted brassicas and they will continue to feed on them right through the winter months, while bullfinches gobble spring blossom and many birds love ripe fruit.

You can use netting, flappers made from strips of strong plastic tied on to lengths of string, dangling DVDs on strings, bottles on canes, and tape that hums, but there's a lot to be said for the old-fashioned scarecrow, which acts as a great deterrent.

With roughly human proportions, and decked out in clothes, these creations will deputise as a gardener when the real ones are indoors, and they work very well, provided your scarecrows are moved around from time to time to trick the birds. They aren't difficult to make and you can opt for either a scary or a friendly version; they're a bit of fun too, and friends soon get used to the sight of an odd character lurking among the vegetables.

You will need

For SCARECROW ONE (or 'terrify-a-crow' as the family call this one!)

- **Timber**
  - 1 x 190cm long, 30mm diameter (75in x 1¼in) pole
  - 1 x 130cm long, 30mm diameter (51in x 1¼ in) pole
- **Pillowcase**
- **Buttons**
- **Felt or strong material**
- **Thread**
- **Wool**
- **Straw, hay, or rag for filling**
- **String**
- **Hat and old clothes**

TOOLS
- Needle
- Saw
- Strong loppers

Making Scarecrow One

STEP 1 MAKE A POINTED END

Use a hand axe to cut a point at one end of the long pole. Take care when doing this: wear protective eyewear and keep your fingers out of the way. Alternatively, use a strong pair of loppers to create a point by nipping off bits around the edges.

STEP 2 TIE POLES TOGETHER

Tie the short pole across the long pole with string to make a cross. The proportions should equate to arms, head and lower body. Decide on clothing at this stage: you may need to thread the sleeves onto the crosspiece now, before tying the two poles together.

STEP 3 STUFF THE HEAD

Tie the top of the pillowcase with string and stuff filling inside. Pat the 'head' into the shape you want before tying the bottom (loosely so the pole will fit – see Step 5). Aim for a round head shape, or for a more realistic look, sew a face-shaped bag to stuff.

STEP 4 CREATE A FACE

Sew on buttons for the eyes and felt for the lips. Or use a permanent marker to draw on a face. There's plenty of scope for creativity to make the kind of scarecrow you want. Try adding eyebrows, eyelashes, ears, some rosy cheeks and teeth.

STEP 5 MAKE SOME HAIR

Cut wool to lengths of around 30cm (12in) and bunch them together to look like hair. Tie the wool in place around the topknot of the pillowcase. Push the top of the long pole into the head, and tie it firmly to the bottom of the pillowcase to fix in place.

STEP 6 DRESS THE SCARECROW

Dress your scarecrow in old clothes and add a hat to cover the topknot. Make sure the garments are tied or pinned in place so they won't blow away. Push the pointed end of the pole into the ground to position the scarecrow.

EXPERT TIP

A front-opening shirt is the easiest clothing option for your scarecrow.

Making Scarecrow Two

You will need

For SCARECROW TWO (the happy one!)

- **Timber**
  - 1 x 200cm long, 50mm x 25mm (79in x 2in x 1in) upright
  - 1 x 80cm long, 50mm x 25mm (32in x 2in x 1in) for shoulders
  - 2 x 40cm long x 50mm x 25mm (16in x 2in x 1in) for lower arms
  - 1 x A4 sized piece of 9mm (³/₈in) plywood, MDF, or similar
- **Screws**
  - 2 x 4mm x 25mm (No 8 x 1in)
  - 4 x 4mm x 40mm (No 8 x 1½in)

TOOLS

- Paper and pen
- Screwdriver
- Drill with 4mm (⁵/₃₂in) drill bit
- Countersink bit
- Sanding sheet
- Jigsaw
- Permanent marker
- Hat and old clothes for dressing
- A few tufts of hay for the authentic look!

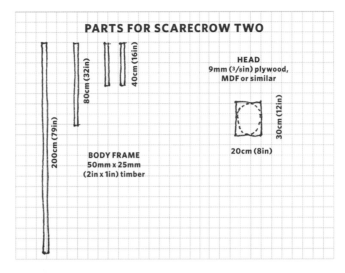

PARTS FOR SCARECROW TWO

200cm (79in)

80cm (32in)

40cm (16in)

BODY FRAME
50mm x 25mm
(2in x 1in) timber

HEAD
9mm (³/₈in) plywood,
MDF or similar

30cm (12in)

20cm (8in)

STEP 1 PREPARE THE TIMBER LIMBS

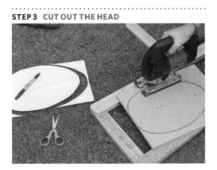

Cut corners off the ends of the lower arm and shoulder timbers. Sand all edges. Cut a point at one end of the upright timber. Use the drill bit and countersink to make clearance holes in the shoulder timber where the body and arms will be joined.

STEP 2 CREATE THE ARMS AND BODY

Allow enough timber above the shoulder for the head to fit. Fix the 200cm and 80cm (79in and 32in) pieces together with two 4mm x 40mm (No 8 x 1½in) screws. Use the other two screws at each elbow joint: allow some slack so they can articulate.

STEP 3 CUT OUT THE HEAD

Draw the shape of the head on a piece of paper. Cut this out and use it as a template to draw around. Mark the head on the plywood (or other sheet material). Support the plywood and clamp it tightly, then cut out the head with a jigsaw.

STEP 4 FIX ON THE HEAD

Use the 4mm (⁵/₃₂in) drill bit to make two clearance holes through the plywood. Fix the head to the top of the upright using two 4mm x 25mm (No 8 x 1in) screws: these pull into the surface a little. Use a thick permanent marker to draw on a face.

STEP 5 DRESS AND PUT IN PLACE

Choose old clothes and use drawing pins or a staple gun to fix them onto the wood or tie on clothes so they won't blow away. Tie a hat on top and poke some hay out of the clothes to give this scarecrow a more traditional look. Secure it in the ground.

USING YOUR SCARECROW

Position your finished scarecrow in the middle of any crop that you want to protect and push the spike deep into the ground so it won't fall over in strong winds.

A helper in the polytunnel will prevent birds stripping off ripening grapes.

- **Move the scarecrow** around the garden or add a different hat, shirt or feature from time to time. Birds can get used to a stationary figure, so moving the scarecrow and mixing things up by adding brightly coloured ribbons or DVDs tied to an arm helps to keep them away.
- **Check the clothes** you intend to use before the frame is assembled. It is difficult to fit the arms of a jumper over a rigid cross, so you may find a shirt much easier. You can also create a more fully formed figure by stuffing hay into sleeves and the legs of the trousers and tying the ends to keep it in place.
- **Use a scarecrow** to keep pigeons off cabbages, cauliflowers and broccoli. Also stand one or more in an orchard to protect apples and pears, or put one in the middle of a soft fruit bed.
- **In the greenhouse**, a strategically placed scarecrow can help to prevent birds from flying in to steal early strawberries or grapes from a vine. One of these figures can also help to stop birds pecking through a polythene polytunnel as they try to get at insects clustered beneath the frame.
- **Involve the children** when making a scarecrow. It is such a fun project and allows children to use their hands and imaginations. Choose an outrageous outfit; give the scarecrow a name and put surprises in the pockets from time to time. You'll soon charm a young generation of gardeners to help in the vegetable patch.

Another scarecrow in the veg patch will guard crops, such as brassicas, including cabbages and purple sprouting broccoli (right), as well as soft fruits.

Wooden planter

Make your own planters using this simple technique to fill your garden and patio with fruit, vegetables and flowers. You can make different sizes to suit your space and then decide what to sow and grow.

Planters allow you to use all available space for a range of flowers and crops.

You will need For a 61cm x 25cm (24in x 10in) planter

- **Timber**
  - 2 x 61cm x 15cm x 25mm (24in x 6in x 1in) sides
  - 2 x 20cm x 15cm x 25mm (8in x 6in x 1in) ends
  - 1 x 56cm x 15cm x 25mm (22in x 6in x 1in) base
  - 2 x 18cm x 50mm x 25mm (7in x 2in x 1in) rails
- **Screws**
  - 16 x 4mm x 40mm (No 8 x 1¹/₂in) screws, stainless steel

TOOLS
- Tape measure
- Saw
- Ruler
- Pencil
- Screwdriver
- Sanding sheet
- Drill with 4mm (⁵/₃₂in) and 10mm (³/₈in) drill bits

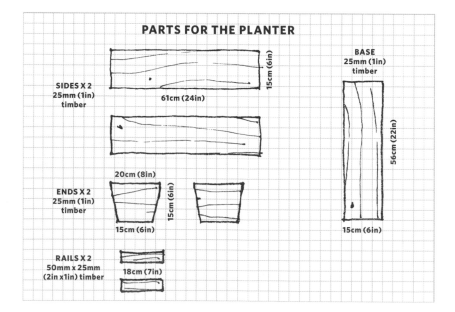

PARTS FOR THE PLANTER

SIDES X 2
25mm (1in)
timber

61cm (24in)

15cm (6in)

BASE
25mm (1in)
timber

56cm (22in)

15cm (6in)

ENDS X 2
25mm (1in)
timber

20cm (8in)

15cm (6in)

15cm (6in)

RAILS X 2
50mm x 25mm
(2in x1in) timber

18cm (7in)

There are lots of beautiful ceramic pots and large containers for sale and these look lovely when planted with a mix of flowers and edible crops. Planters can transform the front of a house or a small patio, creating a beautiful and practical miniature productive garden for very little effort.

Containers can be expensive, of course, but it is really very easy to make your own for much less. You won't require many tools, nor do you need to be a skilled craftsperson to follow this simple design, and you can make larger or smaller versions to suit specific plants. These wooden planters are made from durable larch and look great dotted among ceramic pots, and because they cost so little you may decide to make a whole range to dress up your plot. They're ideal for growing salad leaves, herbs, peas, and strawberries, or any other compact crop that thrives in a confined space.

Making the wooden planter

STEP 1 PREPARE THE TIMBER

Cut timber to the lengths shown on p.60. Keep square ends for the simplest construction, or mark and cut the upright sides at an angle to make a broad wedge shape. Those shown here taper from 20cm (8in) at the top to 15cm (6in) at the base.

STEP 2 DRILL HOLES IN THE SIDES

For both sides, use a 4mm (^{5}/$_{32}$in) bit to make a clearance hole, 15cm (6in) from the end and 12mm (^{1}/$_2$in) from lower edge. Also make one clearance hole at each corner, 12mm (^{1}/$_2$in) from the end and 25mm (1in) from the top and bottom.

EXPERT TIP

When fitting the planter together, remember the sides overlap the ends.

STEP 3 DRILL HOLES IN THE BASE

Use the 10mm (^{3}/$_8$in) drill bit to make 12 holes in the base, spaced evenly at about 30mm (1^3/$_4$in) from the edges. These allow for drainage while not compromising the strength of the base. Sand rough edges and drill holes to remove splinters.

STEP 4 JOIN SIDE AND END PIECES

Lay the pieces out and check they will fit together exactly before assembling. Use 4mm x 40mm (No 8 x 1^1/$_2$in) screws to fix the sides and ends; drive them through the holes drilled in the corners of the sides (see Step 2) and into the end pieces.

STEP 5 ATTACH THE BASE AND RAILS

Slot the base into the frame, so it is flush with the sides. Use two screws through the holes in the lower edges of the sides to fix the base in place. Use the 4 mm (^{5}/$_{32}$in) bit to make clearance holes in the rails. Screw rails in place across the base.

STEP 6 FILL WITH COMPOST

Turn the planter the right way up. It should stand level on the rails. Fill with compost or a mix of compost and well-rotted manure and water well, so the compost is damp enough to plant into. The rails will lift up the planter to allow free drainage.

GROWING TIPS FOR WOODEN PLANTERS

You can use a stain or paint the planter, or leave the wood untreated, but if you want a natural look, use a durable wood such as larch, cedar or oak.

Peas will grow well in these planters.

- **Keep the planter** near a house wall, which will provide a bit of extra warmth and some protection from wind.
- **Remember to water** your container regularly and don't let the compost dry out. Water every day in hot sunny weather.
- **Compost** will contain enough nutrients for roughly six weeks' of strong growth. After this time, use liquid feeds every week to ten days for large plants, or every two weeks for salad leaves.
- **Peas grow well** in this size of planter and will produce a surprising number of pods. Although tall varieties won't reach the heights of those grown in a garden bed, they will flower prolifically at a lower height. Put 12 plants in a planter of this size and push sticks in to support them as they start to climb.
- **Sit the planter** on a low patio wall and grow three strawberry plants. The fruit will tumble down the wall and you can pick and eat it while you sit in the sun.
- **Sow rocket** at any time of the year for a handy supply of this popular salad leaf. Keep plants watered and pick the leaves regularly so plants continue to produce more crops and don't bolt.
- **Grow herbs** by the kitchen door in your planter and you will only have to reach out to pick a few fresh leaves.
- **Make larger planters** for containerised fruit trees, or use them to grow a few salad potatoes, carrots, or beans. Also try flowering bulbs and bedding plants, or anything you like; just ensure you provide enough damp compost and nutrients to sustain good growth.

Support pea stems with twiggy sticks.

The timber colour will fade if left untreated.

Raspberry wire support

Keep your raspberry patch in order with this simple post-and-wire structure. It will restrict the fruit to a defined area, ensure canes grow upright, and allow you to cover the bed easily with netting. The frame also works well for loganberries, blackberries and grape vines.

Raspberries are an easy fruit to grow. They like a slightly acid soil, an occasional feed, a bit of pruning and, of course, you must pick and enjoy the fruit. If left to their own devices, raspberry plants will send out suckers and push up new canes over a wide area. This may suit people with large gardens who don't mind an impenetrable and ever-expanding raspberry bed, but most of us prefer to keep our raspberry rows in check.

The best way to do this is to make a structure that will last as long as the productive life of the plants. The wires for this support are stretched between timber posts and the canes are tied in at appropriate heights. You can dig up suckers that pop up beyond the desired limit of the row and replant them if required, but the idea is to reduce spread and to keep the plants growing along the support wires.

Making the raspberry support

Mark a depth line 40cm (16in) from the pointed end of each fence post. Then mark a drilling point 33cm (13in) above the depth line, plus three more drilling points 33cm (13in) apart above this; the fourth point will be 8cm (4in) below the top.

STEP 2 DRILL HOLES

If the raspberry bed is level, clamp each post firmly and use the 6mm (1/4in) drill bit to make holes through the posts at the points marked in Step 1. If the bed is uneven, or on a slope, leave drilling until the posts are in position (see Step 5).

STEP 3 MAKE HOLES FOR POSTS

Make holes in the ground with a crowbar to accommodate 40cm (16in) of each post. You will need a hole at each end of the row and at evenly spaced distances, about 120cm (48in) apart, in between (closer if supporting individual plants).

STEP 4 KNOCK POSTS IN PLACE

Stand on something steady and use a sledgehammer to knock the posts in place. The posts should be vertical, firmly set in the ground and in a straight line. Stand at one end, look along the row and knock down any posts that are above the rest.

STEP 5 DRILL HOLES (FOR BEDS ON SLOPES)

For beds on uneven surfaces, mark a drilling point 33cm (13in) above ground level and three more, 33cm (13in) apart, above this one. Repeat on all posts. Use a 6mm (1/4in) bit to drill through the posts at the marked points, keeping the drill level.

STEP 6 CUT AND THREAD THE WIRE

Stretch out wire to the length of the frame and allow about 15cm (6in) extra beyond each end post. Use pliers to cut to length. Thread the wire through the lowest holes in all the posts. Repeat with the other wires until all four are threaded through.

STEP 7 FIX ENDS OF THE WIRE

Bend each wire down against the end post and fix with a staple; fold the wire back so it can't pull out. Pull the wire tight through the holes and fix the other end in the same way. Use pliers to trim excess. Repeat with all four wires and aim for an even tension.

STEP 8 TIE CANES TO WIRES

You can use wire ties, clips, or soft string to tie in the raspberry canes. These will only remain in place for a year or less, until old canes are removed. Spread the fruit canes out as evenly as possible, and tie tall ones to more than one wire.

STEP 9 ADD NETTING

Stand back and admire your handiwork! As fruit starts to form, you can throw some bird-proof netting over the top and weigh it down at the edges where it touches the ground with stones or bricks. The posts help to lift the netting above the canes.

PLANTING AND GROWING TIPS FOR THE RASPBERRY SUPPORT

This wire and post system is strong enough to train and support rows of raspberries, but you could also use it for cordon fruit trees.

- **You can make** this frame without drilling holes if you don't have a suitable drill: simply wrap the wire around each of the posts and fix it firmly in place with fencing staples.
- **The best time** to make a frame is when the raspberry bed is first set up. That way you can plant along the frame for an even distribution of canes. Winter is a good time to make the support for established beds because you won't be battling with lots of extra foliage. Having said that, you will see that this frame was put up in spring when the canes were just bursting into leaf – it replaced an old one in our garden and this was the only moment to do it. Because this support is so quick and easy to make, it is better to get on and do it when you are able than to delay and leave the bed to become too wild to tame.
- **Try to set out** your raspberry rows in a direction that affords the plants plenty of sun, which will encourage the formation of plump, sweet fruits.
- **Dig manure** or compost into the ground a week or two before planting the raspberry canes. Add a scatter of potash-rich feed, such as seaweed, at the same time.
- **Plant raspberries** from late autumn until mid-spring, but not when the ground is frozen or waterlogged.
- **Allow 30cm (12in) between canes**, spread the roots out when planting, and cover them with 8cm (3in) of soil.
- **Cut the canes** back to about 23cm (9in) after planting and remove any flowers so that plants will not fruit in their first season, but put all their energy into making strong roots and growth.

This system can also be used for young vines.

Raspberries ripen well when spread out on a frame.

Two-metre square (6ft x 6ft) bed

Easy to make, this 2m x 2m (6ft x 6ft) raised bed is large enough for a whole range of crops, and you can reap the rewards over many months or even all year round if you plan carefully.

There's a garden revolution going on and it starts with the simple idea that we don't have to buy all of our herbs, fruit and vegetables in a shop. A few herbs in a window box are within anyone's grasp, or maybe some vegetables and fruits growing in pots, but here is a way to go a bit further and make a small and highly productive vegetable plot.

Simply follow this step-by-step guide to create and plant up a small bed bursting with food crops. You don't have to make it to the same dimensions, so take what space you have and work with it. You won't become self-sufficient with a plot this size, but if you keep sowing, planting and harvesting, you will always have something to pick, eat and enjoy, even during the winter months.

The starting point is to have the confidence and go for it! Take one raised bed, some plants and a few seeds . . . that's all there is to it.

You will need

For a 200cm x 200cm (72in x 72in) bed

- **Timber decking boards**
  - 2 x 200cm long, 14cm wide, and 32mm thick (72in x 5½in x 1¼in)
  - 2 x 194cm long, 14cm wide, and 32mm thick (69½in x 5½in x 1¼in)
- **Screws**
  8 x 5mm x 70mm (No 10 x 2¾in)
- **Filling**
  Compost, manure, or similar

TOOLS

- Tape measure
- Saw
- Drill with 5mm (³/₁₆in) bit
- Screwdriver
- Sticks and string
- Spade, rake, fork, trowel

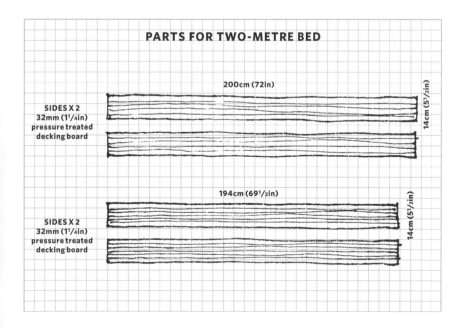

PARTS FOR TWO-METRE BED

SIDES X 2
32mm (1¼in)
pressure treated
decking board

200cm (72in)

14cm (5½in)

SIDES X 2
32mm (1¼in)
pressure treated
decking board

194cm (69½in)

14cm (5½in)

Making the square bed

STEP 1 PREPARE THE BED

Choose a dry day when the soil isn't too wet. Mark out the bed with sticks and string to your chosen size and measure so diagonals are equal. Use a spade to cut along the edges. Dig out perennial weeds and turn grass turves over to reveal the soil.

STEP 2 CUT TIMBER TO SIZE

Saw timber to the lengths you need to fit the bed, or follow the timber list on p.69 for a bed 2m x 2m (6ft x 6ft). Longer lengths overlap shorter lengths, so the bed is square, but you don't need to be too precise, provided the frame fits the space.

STEP 3 ASSEMBLE THE FRAME

Use the 5mm ($^3/_{16}$in) bit to make two clearance holes 15mm ($^5/_8$in) from each end of long timbers. Drive 5mm x 70mm (No 10 x 2$^3/_4$in) screws through holes and into the end grain of the short timbers. Ensure the frame is square; tighten screws.

STEP 4 POSITION AND FILL THE FRAME

Set the frame in place over the dug out bed. Adjust the edges of the bed to get a neat finish, and then fill it with manure and compost, burying the upturned grass turves. Finish with a layer of fine compost and level off with a rake.

STEP 5 FIT CLIMBING SUPPORTS

If the bed is against a fence or wall, use it for climbing plants. We stapled a plastic mesh support against the fence and used this for growing peas of both edible and flowering varieties. Attach any bought support, net, or strings, in a similar way.

STEP 6 DECIDE WHAT TO GROW

This bed was planted with peas, climbing French beans, spinach, rocket, mixed salad leaves, lettuces, courgettes, pattypan squash, strawberries, chives, thyme, sweet marjoram and golden oregano, plus ornamental sweet peas and hollyhocks.

STEP 7 START PLANTING

Mid-spring is a good time to start planting. Sow salad leaves, peas, and beans where they will grow, but buy in a selection of young plants if you want the fastest pickings from a new bed. Protect seedlings and young plants from slugs and snails.

STEP 8 LOOK AFTER YOUR CROPS

Keep the bed watered in dry weather. If you have planted too closely then remove a few plants to allow others to fill out. Keep picking the leafy veg as much as you can to maintain the plants' small size and allow light, air and rain to reach all the crops.

STEP 9 CARE TIPS AFTER 3 WEEKS

If you have a large, early courgette (zucchini) plant, this may produce its first fruits in late spring. Sow some kale, Swiss chard and spinach seeds in pots at this time, so new plants are ready to replace old ones a little later in the summer.

STEP 10 HARVEST 6 WEEKS AFTER PLANTING

Cover your strawberries and other fruit crops with a net if birds are a problem, and pick as soon as the berries are ripe. Plants need plenty of water while the fruits are swelling so ensure you set aside time to irrigate them. Keep picking salad leaves, courgettes (zucchini), herbs, and spinach if you want to get the best crop from each plant. Sow more lettuce seed in pots in early summer to sustain your supply.

STEP 11 HARVEST AND PLANT AFTER 9 WEEKS

Train peas and sweet peas up trellis supports on fences and walls and encourage climbing beans to twine around homemade cane tripods. Clear any rows of spinach, lettuce and rocket that have started to bolt and replant with more of the same, or make space for some kale plants. Continue to pick sweet peas, herbs, and lettuce leaves as you need them.

STEP 12 HARVEST AND PLANT AFTER 12 WEEKS

Keep picking pea pods, as this encourages plants to form more. Try to keep everything under control and ensure the plants are not too crowded at this point. Let squash ramble out of the bed and move finished strawberry plants to pots or a quiet area of the garden. Harvest other crops regularly, and put in new plants, such as kale, lamb's lettuce, rocket, chard and spinach, as old ones are cleared.

SOWING AND GROWING IDEAS FOR THE TWO-METRE SQUARE BED

A small square bed will produce lots of food, but the secret to success is to keep clearing crops and replanting with new ones as the weeks move on.

ABOVE Four tall canes make a pyramid for climbing French beans.
OPPOSITE Remove old plants and replace with new ones to maintain productivity.

- **Peas** should be planted 5cm (2in) apart in a double row. If you have several small plants in one pot, tip out the root ball and plant straight in.
- **Climbing French beans** make a good centrepiece for the bed. Tie four canes together at the top and place them 40cm (16in) apart at the base to form a square. Grow two plants up each cane.
- **Spinach** plants are set out in rows or dot them around to fill empty spaces. Allow 15cm (6in) between plants.
- **Rocket** and **mixed salad leaves** are sown in a shallow drill. Spread a pinch of seed every 45cm (18in) along the row.
- **Lettuce** plants are often grown as a mix of varieties. Eight plants will supply plenty of pickings over several weeks. Set plants 15cm (6in) apart and firm in the root balls gently.
- **Courgette** (**zucchini**) plants are greedy, so dig a 30cm (12in) square hole and fill it with compost. Plant out after the risk of frost has passed.
- **Pattypan squash** are easy to grow from seed in a 25cm (10in) pot. Plant out as for courgette (zucchini).
- **Strawberry** plants grow well in 20cm (8in) pots filled with multi-purpose compost. Sit the pots on the bed if there is room, or line them up along one side.
- **Herbs** grow well in large pots, but they need less watering if they are planted in the raised bed. Grow plants near the edge of the bed, so they are easy to reach and receive plenty of light.
- **Try summer and autumn sowings** of winter lettuce varieties, mizuna, mibuna, mustard greens, corn salad, winter turnips, spinach beet, autumn-planting onion sets, garlic, and spring cabbage plants.

Dot spinach plants in any empty spaces to fill the gaps.

Sow salad leaves in drills at the front of the bed.

Hanging shelf for a polytunnel

It makes a lot of sense to fit some shelves in a polytunnel and utilise the space above low-growing crops. Seedlings can also be grown on them out of the reach of pests, and they allow you to squeeze even more fruit and veg under cover.

A polytunnel is a fantastic growing aid that allows you to produce a wide range of crops throughout the year. But how well do most gardeners fill the available space? Of course, tall crops, such as tomatoes and sweetcorn, will occupy every inch, right up to the roof, but lower-growing crops leave plenty of unused headroom.

The best way to use this empty space is to fit a few hanging shelves. You can use them to raise perfect pea and bean seedlings, or enjoy slug-free ripe strawberries dangling from pots set along a set of shelves.

The shelf shown here is easy to make and install, and you can change the length to fit between the hoops of your structure, or move it to a different part of the polytunnel as you rotate your crops around the beds below. To do this, you simply unscrew the clips and attach them to another section of the frame.

You will need

For a shelf measuring 188cm x 22cm (74in x 9in)

- **Timber**
  1 x planed board:
  188cm long, 22cm wide and 2cm thick (74in x 9in x 3/4in)
- **Rope or galvanised wire**
  2 x 140cm long, 5mm diameter (55in x 3/16in), but allow longer
- **Fittings**
  • 4 x jubilee clips
  • 4 x S-shaped hooks (galvanised or stainless steel)

TOOLS

- Tape measure
- Screwdriver
- Drill with 6mm (1/4in) bit, or a little larger than diameter of rope
- Spirit level
- Sanding sheet
- Pencil

Making the hanging shelf

Measure the distance between the hoops of your polytunnel. Ours are 188cm (74in) apart, but structures vary. Cut the timber to your length. Sand rough edges to remove splinters. Don't cut the rope at this stage, as it will be trimmed to length when installed.

Measure 25mm (1in) from each of the edges of the timber shelf and mark these corner points with a sharp pencil. The measurements don't have to be precise and you could do it by eye. Mark points at all four corners of the shelf.

Use a 6mm (¼in) drill bit to make a hole at the marked points at each corner. Keep the drill as vertical as possible and drill all the way through; the safest way to do this is to hold the wood in a clamp. Sand off any rough bits of wood around the holes.

TIPS FOR USING THE HANGING SHELF

You can use your hanging shelf for a range of crops. Start seeds in trays at almost any time of the year, but remember that they will need watering frequently as the air is warmer at higher levels.

You can use tape instead of clips to secure your shelf to the polytunnel hoops.

- **A shelf** is great for summer sowings when the polytunnel is full to capacity with other crops. Try Florence fennel, spring cabbage, Swiss chard, pak choi, kohl rabi and more, to keep you in vegetables for the colder months of the year.
- **Start pea and bean** seeds in deep trays or individual pots of good quality seed compost. Sow autumn-sowing varieties from mid- to late autumn. Place trays on the shelf and cover with a layer of bubble polythene if nights are cold. We had plants survive temperatures of –12°C (10°F) with this treatment.
- **Strawberries in pots** produce lots of ripe juicy fruit when raised on a shelf. Plants get plenty of light and air and are less prone to botrytis (grey mould). Slugs and snails don't present much of a problem either, but you will need to throw a net over the top to protect against birds.
- **Plants on the shelf** benefit from maximum light levels close to the polythene. You may also need a watering can with a long spout to keep them irrigated and ensure you can get to the shelf easily.
- **As a simple alternative** to clips and hooks, you can tie the rope directly around the frame. Wind tape underneath, so the rope can't slide down the frame, and add more tape between the rope and polythene so it doesn't abrade.
- **The length of rope** used at each end will determine how high or low the shelf hangs. It is best to allow plenty of rope initially and cut it to length once the shelf is hanging at the desired height.

STEP 4 THREAD THE ROPE

Push the end of a long piece of rope through one hole, then pass it across the underside of the plank and pull it up through the opposite hole. Do this with a separate length of rope at each end of the plank, but do not trim it off just yet.

STEP 5 FIT JUBILEE CLIPS

To fit the clips, mark two points about 80cm (32in) apart on each polytunnel hoop. Pass the clips around the frame and through one end of a hook, so only the band touches the polythene. Use a screwdriver to tighten the clip and hook securely in place.

STEP 6 TIE ROPE AND LEVEL THE SHELF

Tie loops in one end of each rope and put these over the lower hooks. Pass the other end through the upper hooks and pull down on the ropes until the shelf is level – ask a friend to help you. Then tie the rope to the upper hooks; adjust the clips if necessary.

Basket planters

You will need

For a planter measuring 60cm x 30cm (24in x 12in)

- **Timber**
  20mm x 20mm ($^3/_4$in x $^3/_4$in)
  planed, cut to:
  - 2 each of: 60cm (24in);
    56cm (22in); 52cm (20$^1/_2$in);
    48cm (19in) for the long sides
  - 2 each of: 30cm (12in);
    28cm (11in); 26cm (10$^1/_4$in)
    for the short sides
  - 15 x 25cm (10in) for the base
    of the planter
  - 2 x 48cm (19in) for the feet
    of the planter
- **Panel pins**
  40mm (1$^1/_2$in) galvanised

TOOLS
- Small saw
- Hammer
- Tape measure
- Pencil
- Sanding sheet
- Piece of card for making
  a measuring gauge

These unusual planters are always admired and they make beautiful gifts. An older child will enjoy making a planter and you can also try the variations constructed with hazel sticks if you feel inspired.

Planters give a splash of colour to any garden. They enhance steps, entranceways or paths, and make beautiful features at any time of year. This planter is designed as a small herb bed, but it can also be used to grow salad leaves or flowering plants.

Herbs grow really well as large specimen plants in individual planters, or put a few together in one container and accept that they may eventually outgrow the space, at which point you can simply plant them in the garden or on the allotment. And remember, when one crop or flower is finished, it's easy to remove the contents, top up with compost, and replant.

The following instructions show how to make this herb planter out of sawn timber. It doesn't take much skill, nor do you need lots of tools, and you can also adapt it to make a planter of any shape or size.

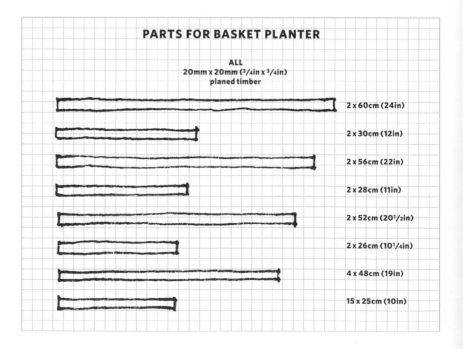

PARTS FOR BASKET PLANTER

ALL
20mm x 20mm ($^3/_4$in x $^3/_4$in)
planed timber

2 x 60cm (24in)

2 x 30cm (12in)

2 x 56cm (22in)

2 x 28cm (11in)

2 x 52cm (20$^1/_2$in)

2 x 26cm (10$^1/_4$in)

4 x 48cm (19in)

15 x 25cm (10in)

Making the basket planters

STEP 1 CUT THE TIMBER AND SAND EDGES

Cut the timbers to length and sand rough edges. A mitre box (see p.28) with a square cut will make this process much easier but it isn't essential. If measuring and cutting without one, simply mark the timber with a pencil and square to give a cutting line.

STEP 2 MAKE A MARKING GAUGE

The sides of the planter taper in even increments; a marking gauge saves time measuring and marking out. Cut stepped notches in a piece of card, marking 1cm (³⁄₈in), 2cm (³⁄₄in) and 3cm (1¹⁄₄in), and use to ensure even insets and overlaps.

STEP 3 ASSEMBLE THE TOP LAYER

The top of this planter has two 30cm (12in) side pieces inset 3cm (1¹⁄₄in) from the ends of the two 60cm (24in) front and back pieces. The side pieces overlap by 1cm (³⁄₈in): use the marking gauge. Ensure the top is square, then fix with panel pins.

STEP 7 FILL THE PLANTER

If you live where there is no shortage of green moss and no legal reason not to use it, then this makes the loveliest lining; if not, buy a basket liner. A hidden sheet of polythene, punctured with a few drainage holes, will help keep the contents moist. Fill the planter with compost.

STEP 4 ADD THE LOWER LAYERS

Nail on the 56cm (22in) and 28cm (11in) pieces for the next layer. Then add the 52cm (20½in) and 26cm (10¼in) timber. Finish off with two pieces of 48cm (19in) along the front and back. Use the gauge to ensure insets and overlaps are correct.

STEP 5 FIX THE BASE RAILS

Fifteen pieces of wood 25cm (10in) long fit across the base like closely spaced ladder rungs. Allow an overlap of 1.5cm (⅝in) at each end and 1cm (⅜in) between rungs. Use a piece of timber to butt them up and fix the rungs in place with panel pins.

STEP 6 ATTACH THE FEET

The last two pieces of wood are 48cm (19in) in length. These fit on the base rungs like the runners on a toboggan. These 'feet' raise the base of the planter off the ground, allowing free drainage. Fix them in place with panel pins.

STEP 8 PLANT WITH HERBS

Three plants will fit nicely into the planter, allowing for some growth; four will give more variety, but they will soon compete for nutrients. Tease free any roots that have wound round in the pot and make sure the compost is damp enough to encourage new root growth.

Hazel planters

Try making beautiful rustic hazel planters using the same method as for the timber types. You will need sticks about 20mm (3/4in) in diameter, sourced from your garden if you have some trees or from coppice craft suppliers. You can also make planters to fit particular areas, such as a slim window box for a narrow sill, or hexagonal planter for a step.

Adding handles to a hazel planter

STEP 1 POSITION THE HANDLE

Lay the planter on its side. Using flexible hazel sticks for the handles, fit one end between two of the rungs that form the base. Fix this end using 30mm (1¼in) panel pins. Bend the handle and fix the other end between two rungs as shown.

STEP 2 FIX THE HANDLES IN PLACE

Aim for a nice even curve. Nail the handle in place at several points, using 30mm (1¼in) panel pins, and saw off any excess that extends below the bottom of the planter. Repeat these steps on the other side for the second handle.

Making a hexagonal basket

STEP 1 MAKE THE SIDES

Lay out a hexagon with alternate, overlapping sticks. Make sure the shape is regular and overlaps are equal before nailing in place. Build up the sides to form a gentle evenly balanced slope, ensuring that the structure doesn't tilt to one side.

STEP 2 FIT THE BASE

Overlapping triangles will close the gap at the bottom of the planter so the contents don't fall out. Alternatively, make straight rungs to fit across the base instead of triangles. Make sure the planter doesn't wobble when standing on a flat surface.

PLANTING AND GROWING TIPS FOR A BASKET PLANTER

Place the planter close to the kitchen door, so you won't have to go out in bad weather to pick a few leaves. Some herbs will provide year-round pickings.

ABOVE Herbs enjoy free-draining conditions so if using a plastic liner, make a few holes in it to allow water to escape.
OPPOSITE These rustic hazel containers make beautiful presents and cost almost nothing if you own a hazel tree.

- **Sprinkle** a little general-purpose organic fertiliser through the compost when planting, or apply a liquid feed after six weeks to top up the nutrients. Feed every few weeks when plants are in active growth.
- **Keep compost damp** and ask a neighbour to take care of watering when you are away.
- **Sow annual** herb seeds, such as basil and coriander, directly into the compost in late spring. Plants should crop for many weeks in summer.
- **Pick regularly** and transplant plants to the garden or a bigger pot before they grow too large and straggly for the size of the planter.
- **In a cold winter**, some perennial herbs, such as rosemary and thyme, do best if they are grown near a house wall for added protection and a little more warmth, or you can bring them into a cool porch. If the compost freezes, bring the planter inside until it thaws.
- **Filled with flowers**, these planters can provide colour through the winter months. Winter-flowering aconites, pansies and snowdrops all look lovely, as do primulas and cyclamens, or try a planter full of indoor hyacinths on a dining table or shelf.
- **You can buy** fresh herbs in pots from many shops. Try a selection in a small planter for a kitchen window ledge. They may not last many weeks, but you will get plenty of leaves in the meantime and plants are within easy reach.
- **Place a tray** under the planter to catch any drips if it is used indoors.

Cherry tree frame

Cherry trees can produce lots of fruit when grown in a fan shape against a sunny wall. This frame supports and trains the tree so it looks tidy, benefits from the extra heat, fruits well, and is easy to prune.

When planting a new tree, choose one that starts branching 30–45cm (12–18in) off the ground. Fit the frame and then train the tree to fan out from this point. If starting with an established unruly specimen that has a longer trunk, then the frame can be fixed up higher. This may not make maximum use of the wall, but you can always train some low branches to fan downwards.

The frame is ideal for fixing to a painted wall: unscrew the upright timbers and tilt them forwards when the wall needs repainting. It's also suitable for a wall made of a hard material because you will only need to drill four holes to fix it to the surface. Make the structure to fit your wall, or to the maximum spread that you want the tree to reach.

You will need

**For a frame measuring
250cm x 100cm (98in x 39in)**

- **Timber**
  - 2 x pressure-treated timbers 100cm long, 45mm wide, and 20mm thick (39in x 1 3/4 in x 3/4in)
- **Bamboo canes**
  - 6 x bamboo canes 180cm (72in) in length
- **Fittings**
  - 10 x 12mm x 75mm (1/2in x 3in) vine eyes, galvanised or stainless steel
  - 4 x 6mm x 50mm (No 12 x 2in) plug-and-screw fixings
- **Wire**
  - 3mm (1/8in) diameter, galvanised
  - Wire ties

TOOLS

- Hammer drill with 6mm (1/4in) masonry drill bit
- 4mm (5/32in) and 6mm (1/4in) wood drill bits
- Pliers
- Screwdriver
- Spirit level
- Hammer and nails
- Tape measure

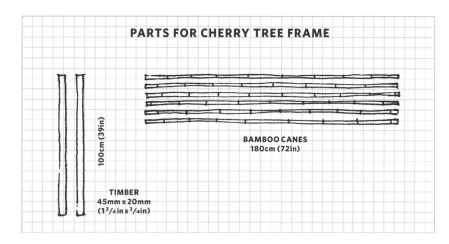

PARTS FOR CHERRY TREE FRAME

BAMBOO CANES
180cm (72in)

100cm (39in)

TIMBER
45mm x 20mm
(1 3/4 in x 3/4in)

Making the cherry tree frame

STEP 1 MARK TIMBER FOR THE FITTINGS

Measure and mark 10cm (4in) from each end of both timbers for the plug-and-screw fixings. Also mark 5cm (2in), 27.5cm (10³/₄in), 50cm (19¹/₂in), 72.5cm (28¹/₂in) and 95cm (37¹/₄in) along the length of each timber for the vine eyes.

STEP 2 DRILL HOLES FOR FITTINGS

Use a workbench or clamp the timbers in a vice. Make holes through each timber with the 6mm (¹/₄in) drill bit at the points marked for the plug-and-screw fixings. Use the 4mm (⁵/₃₂in) drill bit to drill holes at the points marked for the vine eyes.

STEP 3 FIX THE UPRIGHT TIMBERS TO WALL

Hold one timber upright and use a nail to mark the wall through the top plug-and-screw fixing hole. Using the 6mm (¹/₄in) masonry bit, drill a hole here. Hammer a plug-and-screw fixing through the timber into the wall. Repeat with other upright.

STEP 4 ATTACH TIMBERS WITH LOWER FIXINGS

Use a spirit level to make sure the timbers are vertical. Mark the lower plug-and-screw fixing holes as described in Step 3. Use the 6mm (¹/₄in) masonry bit to drill straight through the pre-drilled holes in the timbers, then hammer in the lower fixings.

STEP 5 FIT THE VINE EYES

Screw the vine eyes into all of the pre-drilled holes on each upright. Slide a screwdriver through the eye and use this as a lever when tightening. All vine eyes should lie horizontally, and ensure they don't prise the uprights off the wall.

STEP 6 ADD THE WIRES

Cut wire 30cm (12in) longer than the width between the uprights. Thread through an eye and use pliers to twist and tighten. Pull wire through the corresponding eye on the opposite upright, twist and tighten. Repeat until all wires are fitted; trim with pliers.

STEP 7 POSITION THE BAMBOO CANES

Slide bamboo canes into position. Aim for an even distribution and a good spread over the frame. Rest the canes where they should go, then tie the canes to the wires. Use short pieces of galvanised wire and pliers to fix the canes in place.

STEP 8 TIE THE TREE TO THE FRAME

Start tying in the branches of the tree. Use plastic-covered or rubber flexible tree ties. You can use string, if that is all you've got, but the natural fibres will rot within a few months. Ensure the loops are wide enough to allow the branches to expand.

STEP 9 BALANCE THE SPREAD OF THE TREE

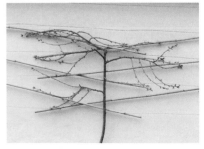

Bend the branches a little to create the spread that you want. Train a few young stems to balance the tree on either side; it is best to do this over a couple of years rather than crack a mature branch. Don't be tempted to prune bare branches.

HOW TO GROW A CHERRY TREE ON A FRAME

This frame will support any fan-trained wall fruit. A warm house wall is ideal for more tender fruits, such as cherry, plum, apricot or peach.

You could choose to dispense with the upright timbers and fix vine eyes and wires directly onto a rustic wall.

- **Put up the frame** when the tree isn't in leaf. This makes it easier to see what you are doing and how the bones of the branches are laid out. It is important not to prune a cherry tree (or a peach, plum, or apricot) in the winter or early spring, as this reduces the chances of diseases entering through the pruning cuts. Instead, simply tie in what you can, and then get out your secateurs from early to midsummer, at which point silver leaf and bacterial canker are less likely to cause problems.
- **Don't worry** if your tree is not perfect. With a small amount of care, you can improve the way it looks and increase its productivity in a relatively short space of time.
- **Choose one book**, or one expert, on fruit pruning; stick to that method and refresh your memory each year before starting to snip. If you hop from expert to expert you may end up with a mix of techniques and, potentially, an unproductive tree.
- **Hang netting** over the frame if birds threaten to eat the ripening fruit.
- **Pick fruit** when it is fully coloured, ripe, and before it starts to crack.
- **To repaint a wall**, fix two temporary pieces of timber horizontally between the two uprights to form a rectangle. You can then unscrew the uprights and ease the frame forwards, just enough to get behind it to paint. Support the frame and take care not to put too much strain on any of the tree's limbs.

Add more supporting canes as your tree grows.

Fruit ripens quickly when grown against a heat-retaining wall.

A-shaped bean frame

An elegant and attractive frame provides a decorative support for climbing beans. This structure is simple and cheap to make, and folds flat when not in use, taking just a few minutes to erect again in late spring.

Climbing beans make a gorgeous feature in any garden. Flowers, foliage and the beans conspire to create a wall of colour, but these climbing plants need a frame to grow up if they are to look their best and crop well. They will also be easier to pick. This A-frame fulfils that function and uses a really pleasing combination of timber and bamboo to enhance the beauty of the beans as they twine around the canes.

The frame fits neatly across the width of a 120cm (48in) bed and is suitable for growing 200cm (79in) tall plants. It is easy to alter the dimensions to make a wider or taller structure, if this better suits your preferred length of row or the height of your favourite variety of beans.

The frame is sturdy enough to support mature plants and it has remained steady through two years of windy weather in our garden.

You will need

For a bean frame measuring 190cm x 100cm (75in x 40in)

- **Timber**
  4 x 230cm long, 50mm wide, 25mm thick (90in x 2in x 1in)
  4 x 90cm long x 50mm wide x 25mm thick (36in x 2in x 1in)
- **Bamboo canes**
  8 x 200cm (78in) long
- **Fencing staples**
  16 large galvanised
- **Butt hinges**
  2 x 10cm (4in) brass with screws
- **Screws**
  16 x 5mm x 80mm (No 10 x 3/4in) stainless steel

TOOLS
- Saw
- Tape measure
- Drill, with 5mm (3/16in) drill bit
- Screwdriver
- Hammer
- Pencil
- Square or a mitre block

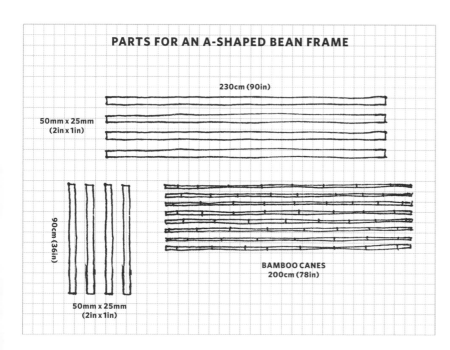

PARTS FOR AN A-SHAPED BEAN FRAME

230cm (90in)

50mm x 25mm
(2in x 1in)

90cm (36in)

50mm x 25mm
(2in x 1in)

BAMBOO CANES
200cm (78in)

Making the A-shaped bean frame

STEP 1   CUT THE TIMBER TO LENGTH

Use the square to mark cutting lines on the lengths of timber. Allow for a 2mm (^{3}/$_{32}$in) wide cut between each piece. Use the saw to cut out the four uprights and four crosspieces: a mitre block will help. Set the timbers with their short edges facing up.

STEP 2   DRILL CLEARANCE HOLES IN UPRIGHTS

Use the 5mm (^{3}/$_{16}$in) drill bit to make two clearance holes, 15mm (^{1}/$_2$in) and 35mm (1^1/$_2$in) from the end of each of the 230cm (90in) pieces of timber. Drill two clearance holes 42cm (16^1/$_2$in) and 44cm (17^1/$_4$in) from the other end of each piece.

STEP 3   ASSEMBLE THE TWO SIDES

Use 5mm x 80mm (No 10 x ^{3}/$_4$in) screws to fix a 90cm (36in) timber as a crossbar between the drilled points at the top of two uprights. Fix a second crossbar between the drilled points 40cm (16in) from the base. Repeat to make two frames.

STEP 4   FIT THE HINGES

Lay your two rectangular frames (each with 40cm (16in) 'legs') together so the top crossbars are square and flush. Leave a small gap between the crossbars, so the hinges don't bind when closed. Screw the hinges in place 15cm (6in) from each end.

STEP 5   ATTACH THE BAMBOO CANES

Place the frame on the ground. Lay four equally spaced bamboo canes across one side. Hammer staples around the canes at the top and bottom to secure them. Allow the canes to overlap or trim to fit. Turn the frame over and repeat on the other side.

STEP 6   PUT THE FRAME IN PLACE

If the ground is hard, use a crowbar to make holes for the legs. Push the legs about 35cm (14in) into the ground, until the frame is straight and level. If you stand on the lower crossbar to push the frame down, do this with great care to ensure it doesn't break!

SOWING AND GROWING TIPS FOR THE BEAN FRAME

Allow one runner bean plant per cane and one for each upright timber, giving you six on each side of the frame. French beans have lighter foliage, so you could put two plants next to each cane.

Bean stems twist in an anticlockwise direction around the canes.

- **Climbing French beans** and runner beans both perform well on this sturdy structure.
- **Dig plenty of garden compost** into the ground before putting up the frame. Alternatively, make planting holes around the frame once it is erected and fill these with compost before planting.
- **Sow seeds** 25mm (1in) deep at the base of each cane, or raise plants in pots and plant out the strongest ones. Sow two weeks before the last frost is expected, as temperatures below 6°C (40°F) can kill plants.
- **Tie in stems** to the canes using soft twine initially to help the tips find their way. Make sure you twist the stems in an anticlockwise direction; they will unravel if they are wound clockwise.
- **Plants grow quickly** and soon start to twist around the canes; when they start twining they will grow and climb on their own without help.
- **Keep the ground** watered in dry weather, especially when the beans are in flower. This stimulates more flowers to set pods.
- **Mist the flowers** with water in hot, dry weather to aid pod set.
- **Pick pods** while they are young and beans are tender. Older beans can be tough and starchy.
- **Put spent plants** on the compost heap in the autumn when cropping is finished. Ensure the frame is dry before folding it flat and storing it in a shed for use the following year.

The frame remains strong and steady when laden.

Plants can be started in pots or tubs indoors in spring.

Timber raised beds

Raised beds are in big demand and it's easy to see why. With just a few timber boards and some bark chip pathways, you can transform the scruffiest vegetable patch into a decorative productive garden.

The appeal of raised beds lies in their neat, structured look, and the fact that they are closer to hand and easier to work than gardening 'on the flat'. You can also build up a good depth of fertile soil and control its acidity (pH) quite easily with the right type of growing medium.

Make the beds to a height that suits you. Some people choose low walls to simply mark out the beds and raise soil levels slightly; others prefer high walls so they don't have to bend much, or for decorative purposes (see p.95 for a tall herb bed). The bed here is 30cm (12in) high, which provides a good soil depth without requiring too much extra material to fill it up.

Choose strong durable timber, such as oak, or the European larch shown here, if you want to leave the wood untreated with a natural appearance. Soft woods, such as spruce or pine, will require a timber preservative.

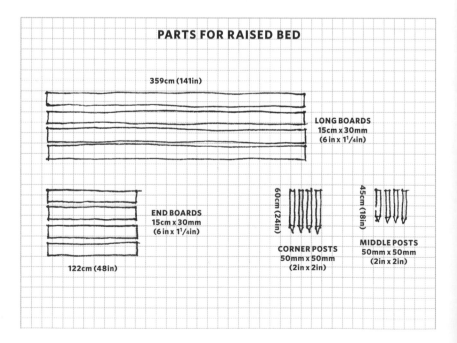

PARTS FOR RAISED BED

359cm (141in)

LONG BOARDS
15cm x 30mm
(6 in x 1¼in)

END BOARDS
15cm x 30mm
(6 in x 1¼in)

122cm (48in)

60cm (24in)

CORNER POSTS
50mm x 50mm
(2in x 2in)

45cm (18in)

MIDDLE POSTS
50mm x 50mm
(2in x 2in)

Making the raised bed

Clear the area where you want the bed. Dig out any weeds and rake the ground, so the bed will sit level. Also remove soil from the paths that will be formed around the edges of the bed, and place this into the centre of your designated area. Create a rectangle 15cm (6in) shorter than the length and width of the raised bed using the soil you have dug out from the paths.

STEP 2 DRILL CLEARANCE HOLES IN THE TIMBER

At both ends of all the long boards, use the 6mm (¼in) drill bit to make two clearance holes, 2.5cm (1in) from the edge and end of the boards. Then drill two more clearance holes, 122cm (48in) from each end and 2.5cm (1in) from the edge of all the long boards. Also drill two clearance holes 6cm (2¼in) from each end and 2.5cm (1in) from the edges of all the end boards.

STEP 3 FIT THE CORNER POSTS

Line up two long boards and place a corner post underneath, so 15cm (6in) extends above the top edge of the boards and the pointed end extends 15cm (6in) below the bottom edge. Use a scrap piece of wood 0.5cm (³⁄₁₆in) thick as a 'spacer' to create an even gap between the ends of the boards and the post. The gap allows the grain to dry out, so the boards are less likely to rot. Hammer drive screws in place.

STEP 4 POSITION THE SIDES

Fix the middle posts to the long boards by knocking drive screws through the pre-drilled holes. The tops of these posts should be flush with the top of the sides. Use string and sticks to mark out the shape of the bed, and a heavy hammer to knock all the corner and middle posts into the ground to form one side. Repeat with the other side, checking that they are the right distance apart.

STEP 5 ATTACH THE END BOARDS

Use string to check the level of the end boards and check that the sides are vertical. Clamp the end boards in position until they are hammered in place. Each cut end should extend beyond the corner post so it is square and level with the boards that form the longer sides of the bed. Using drive screws, hammer the lower end board in place first, and then fix the upper board above it.

STEP 6 FILL THE BED

Spread out any earth that you piled up at the beginning. You will need extra material to fill the bed. A bed this size requires 1.35 cubic metres (48 cubic feet) of topsoil or composted material to completely fill it, but aim for a level around 8cm (3in) below the top of the bed.

Constructing a herb bed

STEP 1 ASSEMBLE SQUARE FRAMES

Use the 5mm ($^3/_{16}$in) bit to make two clearance holes 15mm ($^5/_8$in) from each end of six of the boards. With 5mm x 70mm (No 10 x 2$^3/_4$in) screws, fix through the drilled holes and directly into the end grain of the undrilled boards. Make three square frames in this way.

STEP 2 FIT CORNER POSTS

Mark and drill two clearance holes on each corner post 45mm (1$^3/_4$in) and 95mm (3$^3/_4$in) from one end. Use 5mm x 60mm (No 10 x 2$^3/_8$in) screws to fix the corner posts in place on the lower and middle frames: these extend 20mm ($^3/_4$in) above the top edge of each of the frames.

STEP 3 ASSEMBLE AND PLANT THE BED

Place one frame in position with the corner posts extending upwards. Fit the middle frame over these posts. Then push the top frame in position over the corner posts on the middle frame. Fill with compost (or a topsoil/manure/compost mix) and plant with herbs such as thyme, chives, parsley, oregano and sage.

You can use similar techniques to make a raised herb bed 90cm x 90cm (36in x 36in)

You will need

- **Timber**
  - 12 x decking boards: 90cm long, 14cm wide, and 32mm thick (36in x 5$^1/_2$in x 1$^1/_4$in)
  - 8 x corner posts: 13.5cm long, 46mm wide, 36mm thick (5$^1/_4$in x 1$^3/_4$in x 1$^1/_4$in)
- **Stainless steel screws**
  - 24 x 5mm x70mm (No 10 x 2$^3/_4$in)
  - 16 x 5mm x 60mm (No 10 x 2$^3/_8$in)

TOOLS
- Tape measure
- Square
- Pencil
- Drill with 5mm ($^3/_{16}$in) drill bit
- Saw

TIPS FOR USING AND GROWING CROPS IN A RAISED BED

You can use your raised beds for growing a wide variety of crops, and if you make three or four, you can rotate them from year to year to prevent soil-borne diseases.

ABOVE Harvesting beetroot from a bed.
OPPOSITE Young leeks and beetroot grow really well in a raised bed.

- **If building more** than one bed, make sure they are all the same height and that the ends line up to form a grid pattern. This is simply a visual thing but creates a neat design.
- **The contents** of the bed will settle as the soil or compost packs down. It is a good idea to add new organic material, such as well-rotted compost, or rotted manure, annually when the beds are not filled with crops. Dig this in, or simply spread over the surface of the soil in the autumn, and try not to walk on the bed.
- **Change the dimensions** of the bed to suit your plot. Make it longer or narrower, but don't make it wider unless you have very long arms to reach in from the sides to weed and tend the centre of the bed.
- **Many crops**, including carrots, parsnips, beetroot, leeks, pumpkins, salad leaves, and cabbages, produce really good harvests in raised beds. Sow parsnips and carrots directly into the bed, but you can start most other crops in pots or modules until they are large enough to plant out.
- **Space plants** at closer distances in a raised bed, so you get more produce from the space. As a rule of thumb, aim for 3/4 of the normal recommended planting distance; the soil depth and fertility allows plants to grow a healthy root system even at these reduced spacings.
- **Potatoes** can present problems when it comes to earthing up or digging, but could easily be grown in a bed of their own.
- **Grow peas and beans** in a single tall row up the middle of the bed to allow access from both sides. Low crops, such as lettuces and radishes, can be used to fill the spaces on either side.

Sow carrots directly in drills filled with leafmould.

Use sawdust or bark chips to create paths between beds.

Decorative obelisk

DIFFICULTY LEVEL ⊕⊕⊕⊕⊕⊕⊕⊕⊕⊕

HOURS TO COMPLETE ⊙⊙⊙⊙⊙⊙⊙⊙⊙⊙

You will need

For an obelisk measuring 180cm x 58cm x 56cm (72in x 23in x 22in)

- **Timber**

  35mm x 18mm (1¹/₂in x ³/₄in) pressure-treated timbers for all sections below.

  - 4 x uprights: 180cm (72in) long
  - 2 x lower horizontal braces: 47cm (18¹/₂in) long
  - 2 x lower horizontal braces: 51cm (20in) long
  - 2 x middle horizontal braces: 32cm (12¹/₂in) long
  - 2 x middle horizontal braces: 36cm (14in) long
  - 2 x top horizontal braces: 16cm (6¹/₄in) long
  - 2 x top horizontal braces: 21cm (8¹/₄in) long
  - 4 x top plinth: 18.5cm (7¹/₄in) long

- **Screws**
  - 12 x 3.5mm x 30mm (No 6 x 1¹/₄in)
  - 20 x 3.5mm x 40mm (No 6 x 1¹/₂ in)

- **Exterior paint or wood stain**

TOOLS

- Saw
- Tape measure
- Drill, with 4mm (⁵/₃₂in) drill bit
- Screwdriver
- Pencil
- Sanding sheet

This obelisk for crops or blooms looks elegant in a flowerbed, at the centre of a potager, or as a feature in the vegetable patch. It is easy to make and you can paint it any colour to match your garden scheme.

Gardeners often make temporary frames to support climbing beans, but a more permanent structure like an obelisk can add a beautiful feature to the garden. Shop-bought alternatives are usually much more expensive than the few materials needed to make one and they will not give the satisfaction that creating your own can bring. So get out your tool kit, buy a few lengths of wood, choose a paint colour to enhance the finished look, and make a start. They are so easy that you may decide to put together two or three more obelisks once the first one is completed. The plinth at the top can also be used to augment the design; try a stone, finial, sculpture, a child's artwork, or even a bowl of seeds to feed the birds.

Pressure-treated timber will ensure this structure lasts for many years, but choose a plant-friendly treatment if possible.

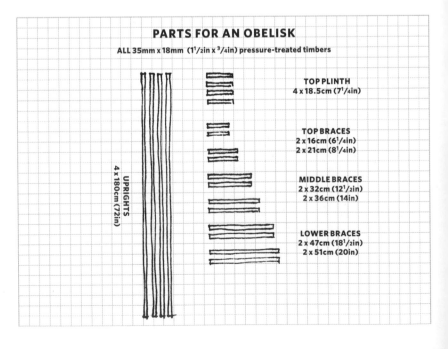

PARTS FOR AN OBELISK

ALL 35mm x 18mm (1¹/₂in x ³/₄in) pressure-treated timbers

UPRIGHTS
4 x 180cm (72in)

TOP PLINTH
4 x 18.5cm (7¹/₄in)

TOP BRACES
2 x 16cm (6¹/₄in)
2 x 21cm (8¹/₄in)

MIDDLE BRACES
2 x 32cm (12¹/₂in)
2 x 36cm (14in)

LOWER BRACES
2 x 47cm (18¹/₂in)
2 x 51cm (20in)

Making the decorative obelisk

STEP 1 CUT THE TIMBER

Cut the uprights; leave one end of each upright uncut, if possible, so the "feet" have a pressure treatment-soaked end-grain. Leave the horizontal braces a little longer than shown: they are cut to the correct angle in Steps 4 and 5, when in place.

STEP 2 MEASURE AND DRILL PILOT HOLES

Mark then drill holes with a 4mm ($^5/_{32}$in) bit: 4cm (1$^1/_2$in) from each end of 51cm (20in), 36cm (14in), 21cm (8$^1/_4$in) pieces; 25mm (1in) from each end of 47cm (18$^1/_2$in), 32cm (12$^1/_2$in), 16cm (6$^1/_4$in) pieces; 1cm ($^3/_8$in) from each end of 18.5cm (7$^1/_4$in) pieces.

EXPERT TIP

Use a timber stain or varnish to finish off the obelisk and reapply every year or two.

STEP 3 ASSEMBLE TWO FRAMES

From the top of each long timber, mark 35mm (1$^1/_2$in), 68.5cm (27in), and 133.5cm (52$^1/_2$in). Fix the braces with 3.5mm x 30mm (No 6 x 1$^1/_4$in) screws: 16cm (6$^1/_4$in) at the top; 32cm (12$^1/_2$in) in the middle; and 47cm (18$^1/_2$in) at the bottom.

STEP 4 TRIM ENDS AT AN ANGLE

Using the edge of the upright as a guide, saw off any surplus timber so the bracing pieces are flush with the uprights. This is an easy way of ensuring that you cut the correct angle on the ends of the bracing pieces. Sand any rough edges.

STEP 5 ASSEMBLE THE FOUR SIDES

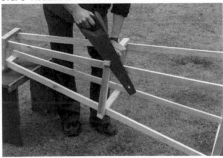

Complete the obelisk sides by fitting the remaining braces using 3.5mm x 40mm (No 6 x 1$^1/_2$ in) screws: these are slightly longer and should overlap the ends of the braces fixed in Step 3. Saw off the overlapping angles (see Step 4).

STEP 6 MAKE THE TOP PLINTH

Use 3.5mm x 40mm (No 6 x 1$^1/_2$ in) screws to fix the four 18.5cm (7$^1/_4$in) pieces evenly across the top. Leave gaps between these slats to allow water to run off. This creates the top plinth when the obelisk is stood upright.

TIPS FOR GROWING CROPS ON THE OBELISK

Set the obelisk in place, allowing enough room to walk round when harvesting, and push the feet down 30cm (12in) into the soil to give it added stability.

Bean stems twist around the legs.

- **Climbing French beans** have lighter foliage than runner beans and hence are a perfect choice for the obelisk: the latter can grow to completely swamp the structure. If you want to grow runner beans, then either choose a short variety or make a taller obelisk!
- **Beans grow best** in a moisture-retentive soil enriched with garden compost. If the bed isn't already prepared in this way, then dig a hole next to each leg and fill with compost before sowing.
- **Sow two beans**, 5cm (2in) deep, next to each leg, plus one or two extras in pots on a window ledge. These surplus plants will help to avoid disappointment: you can plant them out if some of the direct-sown seeds fail to germinate.
- **Growing stems** twine anticlockwise around the legs. Growing tips may need a little help to find the legs and to start twining. Just point them in the right direction until they touch a leg and they should do the rest by themselves.
- **Bean flowers** usually set pods without any trouble, but in very dry weather it is worth giving a light spray of water over the whole plant to aid this process.
- **Try growing sweet peas** or morning glory plants up the obelisk.
- **Small-fruiting climbing squash** look lovely climbing over the obelisk; larger fruits will need some support so they don't break the stems.
- **An egg-shaped** pebble and child's pottery on the plinth became a favourite perch for a robin in our garden. This bird was always ready to eat pests that were uncovered when pots were moved or beds dug over.

Try using the obelisk in your flower borders.

Ring the changes each year by moving the obelisk to a different position.

Multi-purpose boot tool

You will need

For a boot tool measuring 127cm x 36cm x 24cm (50in x 14in x 9in)

- **Timber**
  - 1 x board: 62cm long, 15cm wide, and 2cm thick (24^{1}/$_{2}$in x 6in x ^{3}/$_{4}$in)
  - 2 x legs: 15cm long, 4cm wide, and 4cm thick (6in x 1^{1}/$_{2}$in x 1^{1}/$_{2}$in)
  - 1 x broom handle: 122cm (48in) long
- **Brush heads**
  - 2 x 23cm wide x 70mm high (9in x 2^{3}/$_{4}$in)
- **Screws**
  - 8 x 5mm x 50mm (No 10 x 2in)
  - 4 x 5mm x 70mm (No 10 x 2^{3}/$_{4}$in)
  - 4 x 4mm x 35mm (No 8 x 1^{3}/$_{8}$in)
  - 2 x 5mm x 40mm (No 10 x 1^{1}/$_{2}$in)

TOOLS

- Tape measure
- Screwdriver
- Drill with 5mm (^{3}/$_{16}$in) and 3mm (^{1}/$_{8}$in) drill bits
- Jigsaw or handsaw
- Square
- Pencil
- Sanding sheet
- **Optional**: hand plane, countersink bit

Boot cleaners are hard to find but this clever tool does the job perfectly and takes just a few hours to make. It not only cleans and helps to remove dirty boots, but provides support while you balance on one foot.

Gardeners know all about muddy boots and they also know about hopping around with one foot raised underneath a tap. To solve this problem and take the wobble and mess out of removing dirty boots we have devised this boot cleaning system. You simply hold onto the handle while you put the brushes and V-section to good use.

We have got plenty of use from our practical boot tool, especially since it is kept close to the house door. This project also makes a great gift for any gardening friends; simply double or treble the materials to make a batch, and paint the timber in a pretty shade or leave it natural.

The construction technique is easy for anyone with a few basic tools and it is possible to complete this project in an afternoon. Your local DIY store is the best place to source a selection of brushes and broom handles.

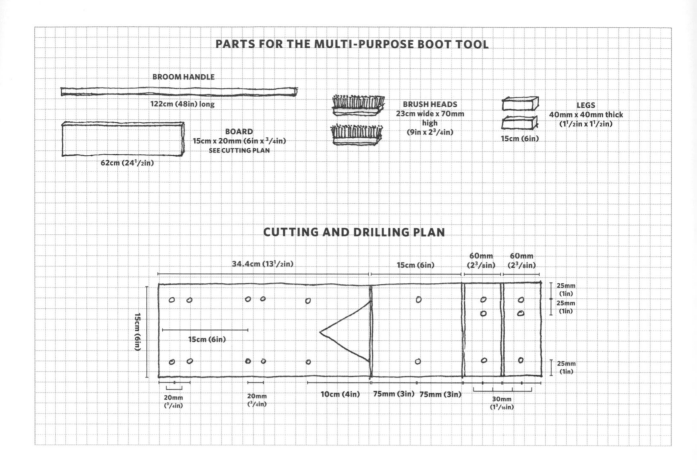

PARTS FOR THE MULTI-PURPOSE BOOT TOOL

BROOM HANDLE
122cm (48in) long

BOARD
15cm x 20mm (6in x ³/₄in)
SEE CUTTING PLAN
62cm (24¹/₂in)

BRUSH HEADS
23cm wide x 70mm
high
(9in x 2³/₄in)

LEGS
40mm x 40mm thick
(1¹/₂in x 1¹/₂in)
15cm (6in)

CUTTING AND DRILLING PLAN

34.4cm (13¹/₂in)   15cm (6in)   60mm (2³/₈in)   60mm (2³/₈in)

25mm (1in)
25mm (1in)

15cm (6in)

15cm (6in)

20mm (³/₄in)   20mm (³/₄in)   10cm (4in)   75mm (3in)   75mm (3in)   30mm (1³/₁₆in)

25mm (1in)

USING THE BOOT TOOL

This tool answers that age-old problem of how to remove dirty boots without mess. You can also augment it with extra scraping devices for large clods of mud.

- **Paint** the boot tool or use an oil or stain to protect the timber. Untreated wood will age gracefully, but it will only last a few years before it starts to deteriorate.
- **Hold the handle** so it is easy to stand on one leg while you line up the other foot on the brushes. This also stabilises the boot tool.
- **Direct a hosepipe** over boots while brushing and give a squirt over the brushes after use; remember to remove any build-up of mud that might clog the bristles.
- **To remove a boot**: stand with the brushes towards you and grasp the handle with both hands. Put one leg forward so the heel of the boot is caught in the V. Pull your leg back towards your body and the boot should slide off easily.
- **This design** could also incorporate a flat piece of metal that protrudes to one side which can be used to remove large clods of mud before using the brushes. Alternatively, you can add an extra piece of wood, cut with a bevel to create a pointed edge, to do the same job. The boot tool works perfectly well without it, but any enthusiastic metalworkers might want to have a go at improving the design.

Making the boot tool

STEP 1 MARK OUT THE TIMBER

Use the square and pencil to mark cutting lines and drilling points on the 62cm (24½in) piece of timber, as shown in the diagram (left). Each saw cut takes up a little timber: allow for this and mark each cut with two lines 2mm (5/64in) apart.

STEP 2 DRILL HOLES

Set the 62cm (24½in) piece of timber on the two legs for support, and use a clamp, so the drill doesn't touch the workbench. Use the 5mm (3/16in) bit to drill all holes marked in Step 1, and a countersink bit to produce a neat finish.

STEP 3 CUT OUT THE V

With the jigsaw or handsaw, cut the 62cm (24½in) piece of timber into four pieces along the lines marked in Step 1. Then cut out the V section. If you have very large boots, you may need to cut a wider and deeper V shape to accommodate them.

STEP 4 SAND EDGES

Use the sanding sheet to smooth all rough edges (wrap the sanding sheet around a block of wood to give a firm flat surface to sand against). Some broom handles are rougher than you may imagine so give them a quick rub down to remove splinters.

STEP 5 MAKE THE HANDLE SUPPORT

The three small, flat pieces of wood hold the handle and the upright brush support. Use 4mm x 35mm (No 8 x 1⅜in) screws to assemble these pieces as shown. Allow enough room for the broom handle to fit snugly into the groove in the middle.

STEP 6 FIX THE HANDLE

Screw the broom handle in place with two 5mm x 40mm (No 10 x 1½in) screws. Make sure the bottom edge of the handle is level with the rest of the block: hold a piece of straight timber across the base to ensure a flush edge.

STEP 7 DRILL PILOT HOLES IN BRUSH HEADS

Use a hand plane to square off any rounded top edges on the brush heads. Make pilot holes in the brush heads with the 3mm (⅛in) drill bit. The holes should correspond to those on the base and upright sections, where the brushes will fit onto them.

STEP 8 FIT THE LEGS AND BRUSHES

Use 5mm x 50mm (No 10 x 2in) screws to fit through the holes in the base board and corresponding 3mm (⅛in) pilot holes in the legs. To fit the brushes, use 5mm x 70mm (No 10 x 2¾in) screws through holes in the base board and handle support.

STEP 9 ASSEMBLE THE BOOT TOOL

Drill four pilot holes into the end of the upright section, corresponding to the remaining holes in the baseboard. Use 5mm x 50mm (No 10 x 2in) screws to fix the upright and base together. Aim for a right angle, so the brush heads line up correctly.

Drying cabinet

Dry your own tomatoes, apples, peppers and pears in this simple cabinet. An easy way to preserve delicious fruit and vegetables, the cabinet will allow you to make your own semi-sundried tomatoes in oil, dried soup mixes for the winter months, and healthy snacks.

Drying is one of the oldest methods of preserving food and it has become a modern favourite too. All that is needed is a constant low heat so food dries slowly, but not so slowly that moulds can grow. There are several ways to do this, and during a long hot summer, sun-drying is an obvious choice. However, many people don't have the reliably hot dry climate that suits this technique, so instead we use a sunny window ledge, buy a dehydrator, or use the lowest setting on the oven with the door slightly ajar. All these methods are effective, but for a simple and cheap option that provides a steady low heat and works reliably well, it's easy to make your own drying cabinet.

Either convert an existing cupboard by drilling holes, fitting a heating lamp and adding wire shelves, or make a cupboard from scratch. Either way, a cabinet offers a dedicated system for use throughout the year.

You will need

For a cabinet to hold five trays measuring 33cm x 27.5cm (13in x 10³/₄in)

- **Plywood**
  12mm (¹/₂in) plywood cut to size and with edges sanded
  - 2 x 97cm x 30.5cm (38in x 12in) for the door and back
  - 2 x sides: 99cm x 40cm (39in x 15³/₄in)
  - 1 x base: 40cm x 28.3cm (15³/₄in x 11¹/₈in)
  - 1 x top: 42.4cm x 30.5cm (16⁵/₈in x 12in)
- **10mm (³/₈in) dowel**
- **5 x wire cooling trays**
- **Fittings**
  - Light fitting
  - 200cm (78in) flex
  - Plug
  - 40W terrarium lamp
  - 2 x 50mm (2in) flush hinges with screws: 12mm (¹/₂in) max to screw into ply
  - 4mm x 30mm (No 8 x 1¹/₄in) screws

TOOLS
- Jigsaw
- Drill with 10mm (³/₈in), 4mm (⁵/₃₂in) and 2mm (⁵/₆₄in) drill bits
- Screwdriver
- Tape measure/rule
- Pencil
- Fine sanding sheet

SCALING YOUR CABINET TO FIT YOUR TRAYS

Source the wire cooling trays first and build a cabinet to accommodate them. Trays vary in size and you will have to alter the dimensions according to the size of those you choose. Measure the length and width of a tray and cut plywood to the system below:

2 x [width of tray + 30mm] x 97cm ([width + 1¹/₄in] x 38in) door and back

2 x [length of tray + 70mm] x 99cm ([length + 2³/₄in] x 39in) sides

1 x [length of tray + 70mm] x [width of tray + 8mm] ([length + 2³/₄in] x [width + ⁵/₁₆in]) base

1 x [length of tray + 94mm] x [width of tray + 30mm] ([length + 3³/₄in] x [width + 1¹/₄in]) top

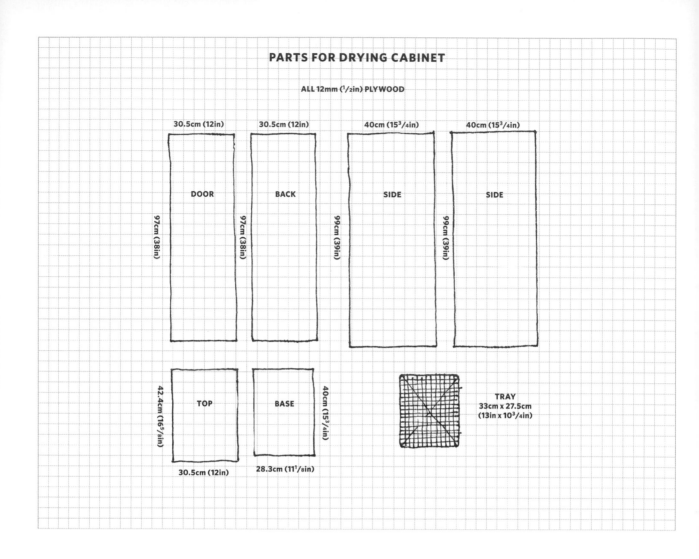

PARTS FOR DRYING CABINET

ALL 12mm (1/2in) PLYWOOD

30.5cm (12in)	30.5cm (12in)	40cm (15³/₄in)	40cm (15³/₄in)
DOOR	BACK	SIDE	SIDE
97cm (38in)	97cm (38in)	99cm (39in)	99cm (39in)

TOP — 42.4cm (16⁵/₈in), 30.5cm (12in)

BASE — 40cm (15³/₄in), 28.3cm (11¹/₈in)

TRAY
33cm x 27.5cm
(13in x 10³/₄in)

Making the drying cabinet

STEP 1   DRILL HOLES TO FIX THE BASE

Draw a line 30mm (1¹/₄in) from the lower edge of each of the two sides. With a 4mm (⁵/₃₂in) bit, drill three evenly spaced holes along each line. Draw a line 10mm (³/₈in) from the lower edge of the back board. Drill three more holes along this line.

STEP 2   FIT THE TRAY SUPPORTS

With a 2mm (⁵/₆₄in) bit, make pilot holes in each of the sides, 8cm (3in) from the long edges. The first set go 33cm (13in) from the base, to allow space for the light fitting, then 10cm (4in) apart. Fix in screws but leave them protruding by 19mm (³/₄in).

STEP 3   MAKE VENTILATION HOLES

Use the 10mm (³/₈in) bit to drill a double row of holes at the top and bottom of the sides of the box. Holes are 5cm (2in) apart and allow 4cm (1¹/₂in) between rows. This makes 14 holes at the top and bottom of each side, and will allow air to circulate.

STEP 4 FIT THE HEAT SOURCE

Use the 10mm (3/8in) bit to make a hole in the centre of the base board. Thread the flex through this. Wire in the plug and light fitting. Use the 2mm (5/64in) bit to make pilot holes and screw the fitting in place. Use a 40W heating lamp.

STEP 5 ASSEMBLE THE SIDES AND BASE

Use the 2mm (5/64in) bit to make pilot holes in three sides of the base into the ends of the ply. Screw the sides onto the base, and the back to the sides, through the pre-drilled holes. The back is shorter than the sides to allow room for flex underneath.

STEP 6 ADD A HANGING RAIL

Use a piece of 10mm (3/8in) dowel to slide between two ventilation holes across the top. Cut to the required length. This step is optional. A rail is useful for hanging herbs or peppers to dry, but if you prefer, fit an extra couple of shelves instead of a rail.

STEP 7 FIT THE TOP

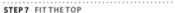

Use the 4mm (5/32in) bit to make holes 6mm (1/4in) from the edge of the top, and the 2mm (5/64in) bit for pilot holes in the ends of the ply sides and back. Screw the top in place. Screws must be vertical, so they go through the middle of the ply ends.

STEP 8 FIT THE HINGES AND DOOR

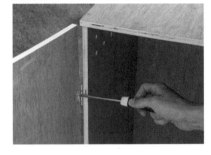

Fix the hinges 15cm (6in) from the top and 15cm (6in) from the bottom of the door. Hold the hinges in place and mark where the screws will go. Use a 2mm (5/64in) drill bit to make pilot holes, and then fit screws. Make sure the door is level and closes well.

WARNING!

Put muslin or kitchen paper on the shelves to absorb any drips from wet fruit. If drips land on a hot light bulb it can shatter!

STEP 9 FIT SHELVES AND FILL IT UP

Fit a catch to the door. You can simply add two screws and a bit of wire to make one. Alternatively buy a magnetic catch, or similar system, from your local DIY store. Slide the shelves into place. Make sure the bulb is fitted before the unit is plugged in.

CLOCKWISE FROM TOP LEFT Make a dried vegetable soup mix; dry different fruits on different shelves; cut small tomatoes in half before drying; use dried apple rings to make a delicious snack; slice fruit thinly and dip in lemon solution.

OPPOSITE Store dried tomatoes with garlic in olive oil; dried pears and strawberries make a tasty treat.

TIPS FOR DRYING FRUIT AND VEGETABLES IN THE CABINET

Use the cabinet to make tasty semi-dried tomatoes in flavoured oils, or try dried fruit rings as a healthy snack for all the family.

- **Apple and pear** flesh turns brown when exposed to air. Dip sliced fruit in a mix of one part lemon juice to two parts water and add a teaspoon of sugar to every half litre (pint). Let fruit drain until it stops dripping before laying the slices on trays in the cabinet.
- **Thin slices** dry much faster than thicker ones. Check regularly and sample a slice or two to make sure they are dried to perfection.
- **Remove the pulp** and seeds from larger tomatoes and cut the flesh into segments to speed up drying. Cut small tomatoes in half with the pulp and seeds left in and sprinkle with salt to improve the flavour. Small pieces like these take 24–36 hours to semi-dry, then store in olive oil.
- **If mould develops** on your fruit or vegetables, you probably don't have enough heat in the cabinet. Use a higher wattage bulb, and make sure the air holes aren't blocked so that air can circulate.
- **If fruit is dry** and crisp then the cabinet is too hot, or you have left the trays in for too long. Use a lower wattage bulb, or remove the contents of the tray sooner.
- **Experiment** until you find what produce tastes best when dried. Also try small quantities until you find perfect drying times for each crop.
- **Eat dried fruits** straight away, or store them in jars until needed. (If fruit is poorly dried it will not store well.)
- **Turn the light off** when the cabinet is not in use.

Poly-cloche frame

Our poly-cloche frame was designed to fit on top of a raised bed to create a protected area for pumpkin plants, but it works equally well on flat ground. The cover opens from one side to allow easy access to the plants.

Pumpkins and squashes are such bright and cheery crops to grow and they store for months over winter. Plants can produce lots of foliage, but if late spring is cooler and wetter than we expect, and the summer months don't show much improvement, we are unlikely to get a bumper crop. A little protection can make all the difference, improving plant growth and fruiting, so the frame seemed like an obvious solution.

This structure is designed to be light enough to lift and put in place, and tall enough to allow plants to grow inside for several weeks. In fact, it has proved to not only work well for pumpkins, but for many other crops that like a protected growing space.

The frame will last for many years if you use pressure-treated timber and replace the polythene every few years as required.

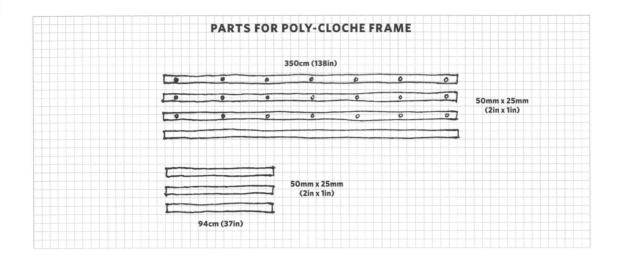

PARTS FOR POLY-CLOCHE FRAME

350cm (138in)

50mm x 25mm
(2in x 1in)

50mm x 25mm
(2in x 1in)

94cm (37in)

Making the poly-cloche frame

STEP 1 MARK AND DRILL HOLES FOR THE PIPE

Mark 6cm (2½in) from each end of one 350cm (138in) timber. Mark five more points 56cm (22in) apart along the length, making seven drilling points. Use a 28mm (1⅛in) bit to make holes at these points. Repeat on two more of the long timbers.

STEP 2 ASSEMBLE THE BASE

Use the 5mm (³⁄₁₆in) bit to drill clearance holes 2cm (½in) and 4cm (1½in) from each end of two long lengths of timber and at the midpoints. Fix three short pieces to make a rectangular frame (as shown) using 5mm x 100mm (No 10 x 4in) screws.

STEP 3 CUT THE PIPE TO LENGTH

With the hacksaw, cut the semi-rigid water pipe into seven equal lengths. This frame uses 163cm (64in) lengths, but if you want a taller or shorter frame, adjust the length accordingly. When cutting, hold the pipe securely in a vice or workbench.

STEP 4 ASSEMBLE THE HOOPS

Push the pipe through the holes in the top rail. Position the rail 10cm (4in) to one side of the midpoint of the pipes, and push the ends into the base. Use a 4mm (⁵⁄₃₂in) bit to fix one 4mm x 25mm (No 8 x 1in) screw into the pipe through the side of each hole.

STEP 5 FIX ONE EDGE OF THE POLYTHENE

Staple one edge of the polythene to the underside of one edge of the base. Or, you can sandwich the polythene between two layers of wood screwed together. Put the frame in position and roll up surplus polythene on the top rail.

STEP 6 TIE THE FRAME TO THE BED

Use washing line or rope to tie the frame in place onto the raised bed. Tie this to the raised posts, through a drilled hole in the side of the bed, or round a fixed cleat. It is important to secure the frame so that it doesn't move in strong wind.

STEP 7 COVER THE FRAME

Unroll the polythene over the top of the frame. Use the last piece of timber to roll up the loose edge and lay it flat on the ground. Staple the polythene to the wood, or fix it between two timbers (see Step 5).

STEP 8 CLOSE THE TWO ENDS

Gather the loose polythene at one end of the frame. Give it a twist and use a heavy stone to weigh it down (as shown) or tie it off with strong string. Trim any excess length of polythene to make a neat closure.

Creating a heated propagator

You can adjust the size of this frame – minus the middle crosspiece – to make a smaller structure to set over a heated mat. The mat is thermostatically controlled to ensure even heat; a bit of extra insulation over the cover on cold nights will help to keep running costs down.

Many propagators are too small to allow anything more than a few centimetres of growth, but this one has plenty of headroom. It is only when plants touch the polythene cover that they need to move out of their starter home.

It is a good idea to buy the thermostatically controlled mat beforehand, so you can build your poly-cloche frame to the right size to fit neatly over it.

STEP 1 SET UP THE HEATED BASE

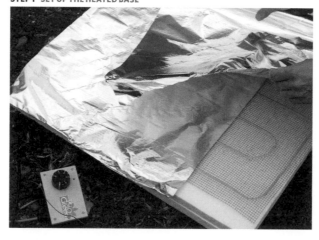

Lay the mat on top of a 5cm (2in) layer of expanded polystyrene insulation board. Cover the mat with aluminum foil and place a layer of strong polythene on top for protection. Pots and trays can then sit directly on top of the polythene sheet.

STEP 2 COVER WITH A FRAME

SAFETY TIP

Plug the propagator into an outdoor socket fitted with a residual-current device (RCD) and ensure cables are suitable for outdoor use.

Make the frame the correct size to sit neatly over the heating base, with a few centimetres to spare on either side. Ensure electrical cables and connections are safe and dry. Set the thermostat to 20°C (70°F) for germinating heat-loving seeds and cover the frame with clear polythene.

SOWING AND GROWING TIPS FOR A POLY-CLOCHE FRAME

You can plant squash, pumpkins and other crops that benefit from extra protection from the elements in spring, or try growing onions over winter.

Open the cloche when squashes are in flower to allow access for pollinators.

- **Use crop-cover** instead of polythene if you want to provide your plants with some protection, but still allow rain and air to penetrate.
- **The strongest polythene** you can buy is best for a long-lasting covering.
- **Let the soil warm up** under the frame for a few days before planting up.
- **Open the ends** to allow extra ventilation on warm days, and on hot days open one side and rest the polythene-rolled timber on the top rail – which is offset so the roll doesn't slip – or roll the cover back completely.
- **Use the frame** to protect winter crops, such as lettuce, rocket, onions, spinach and chard, or to give extra protection to early spring sowings.
- **When pumpkins** or other fruiting crops are in flower, open the frame to allow insects access to pollinate the blooms.
- **Close the poly-cloche** frame at night until temperatures are high enough to maintain healthy growth.
- **Water** plants under the cloche regularly.
- **Remove the frame** when plenty of fruits are swelling on pumpkin plants and move it to another bed if needed. Leave the pumpkins to ramble where they want.
- **If your garden** is exposed to strong winds, use extra weights to hold down the polythene on the opening side of the frame. Use larger-sized timbers along the edge if necessary, or weigh down edges with bricks.
- **Dismantle** the frame and store it in a shed if it isn't needed for a while – simply roll up the polythene, then unscrew and remove the hoops, to create a flat-pack kit.

OPPOSITE Planting out early squash.
RIGHT Over-wintered onions under the frame.

Seed trays, dibber & scraper

A set of handmade wooden seed trays makes a lovely gift, and with a dibber and scraper you can make a practical collection that any gardener will love.

Experienced gardeners will appreciate these sturdy trays, which are designed to fit a desired number of pots without wasting space. The large tray holds twelve 9cm (3½in) square pots and the small tray holds four of the same size. Children will love them too, especially if some packets of sunflower or pumpkin seeds are included in their gift.

A spade scraper is a slightly more advanced project, but anyone who uses a spade will know how to put it to good use. Use the wedge end of the tool to remove any clay or mud after digging heavy ground.

The dibber is a tool that young children will love: push it into compost to make a hole then drop in a seed. Of course a finger will do this job, but there is nothing like a bit of tool magic to hold a young gardener's interest.

You will need

Two trays measuring 42.5cm x 32cm (16½in x 12½in) and 23cm x 23cm (9in x 9in)

- **Timber for large tray, planed**
  - 7 x base slats: 42cm long, 43mm wide, and 17mm thick (16½in x 1¾in x ¾in)
  - 2 x short sides: 32cm long, 43mm wide, and 17mm thick (12½in x 1¾in x ¾in)
  - 2 x long sides: 39cm long, 43mm wide, and 17mm thick (15in x 1¾in x ¾in)
- **Timber for small tray, planed**
  - 5 x base slats: 23cm long, 43mm wide, 17mm thick (9in x 1¾in x ¾in)
  - 2 x short sides: 19.5cm long, 43mm wide, and 17mm thick (7½in x 1¾in x ¾in)
  - 2 x long sides: 23cm long, 43mm wide, and 17mm thick (9in x 1¾in x ¾in)
- **Nails**
  50mm (2in) galvanised ovals
- **Timber for scraper and dibber**
  - 1 x 15cm long, 43mm wide, 17mm thick (6in x 1¾in x ¾in) scraper
  - 1 x 15cm long, 10mm diameter dowel (6in x ⅜in) dibber

TOOLS FOR SEED TRAYS
- Saw
- Hammer
- Tape measure
- Square
- Drill with 3mm (⅛in) drill bit
- Sanding sheet and sanding block
- Pencil
- Matches
- Cardboard 43mm x 17mm (1¾in x ¾in), folded in half across the shorter length

TOOLS FOR DIBBER & SCRAPER
- Cardboard
- Pencil
- Broad bevel-edged (carpenter's) chisel
- Jigsaw or coping saw
- Drill with 8mm (5/16in) bit
- Metal file or sandpaper

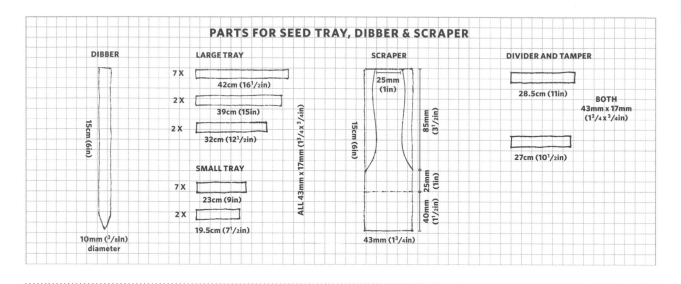

PARTS FOR SEED TRAY, DIBBER & SCRAPER

DIBBER
15cm (6in)
10mm (³/₈in) diameter

LARGE TRAY
7 X — 42cm (16¹/₂in)
2 X — 39cm (15in)
2 X — 32cm (12¹/₂in)

SMALL TRAY
7 X — 23cm (9in)
2 X — 19.5cm (7¹/₂in)

ALL 43mm x 17mm (1³/₄ x ³/₄in)

SCRAPER
25mm (1in)
15cm (6in)
85mm (3¹/₂in)
25mm (1in)
40mm (1¹/₂in)
43mm (1³/₄in)

DIVIDER AND TAMPER
28.5cm (11in)
BOTH 43mm x 17mm (1³/₄ x ³/₄in)
27cm (10¹/₂in)

Making the seed trays, dibber & scraper

STEP 1   MAKE A MARKING CARD

Mark two arrows on one edge of the piece of card, 10mm (³/₈in) from each side. Use this, as shown, to mark drilling points on both ends of all pieces of timber *except* the 39cm (15in) lengths for the large tray and 19.5cm (7¹/₂in) lengths for the small tray.

STEP 2   DRILL CLEARANCE HOLES

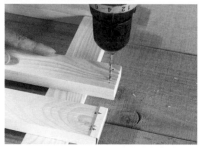

Use the 3mm (¹/₈in) bit to make two guide holes at each end of the timber pieces as marked in Step 1. Support the timber when working so you don't drill straight into the bench. Rub the sanding sheet over all rough edges until they feel smooth.

STEP 3   ASSEMBLE LARGE AND SMALL FRAMES

Nail the frames together through the clearance holes and into the end grain. The 32cm (12¹/₂in) pieces overlap the ends of the 39cm (15in) pieces for the large tray; 23cm (9in) pieces overlap the ends of the 19.5cm (7¹/₂in) pieces for the small tray.

STEP 4   FIT THE BASES

Place the remaining timbers across the base of each tray. Use matchsticks as spacers and nail the slats through the clearance holes, taking care to position the two outer slats so that the nails don't collide with those holding the frame.

STEP 5   SQUARE AND LEVEL THE TRAYS

Blunt the tip of a nail by hammering it lightly against a stone or piece of metal. Use this nail to knock nail heads just under the surface of the timber; protruding nails can scratch surfaces or cut hands. Make sure the two trays are square and sit level.

STEP 6   MAKE THE DIVIDER AND TAMPER

Cut a length of timber 28.5cm x 43mm x 17mm (11in x 1³/₄in x ³/₄in). This will divide the large tray into two sections. Use another length of timber 27cm x 43mm x 17mm (10¹/₂in x 1³/₄in x ³/₄in) to help compact compost evenly across the tray.

Cut a piece of dowel, 10mm ($3/8$in) in diameter, to 15cm (6in). Use a chisel to make a point at one end, or try a pencil sharpener with a large enough cutting hole and a sharp blade. Sand both ends and round off the point to make it blunt.

Cut a template out of card: the one shown here is 15cm (6in) long and the handle is 25mm (1in) at its widest point. You can change the dimensions to suit a large or small hand. Lay the template on the piece of wood and mark around it with a pencil.

With a three dimensional design it is easier to see which areas you need to cut away if you crosshatch them with a pencil as shown, leaving the lines of the scraper easy to see. The tip of the scraper makes an angle over a length of about 40mm (1$1/2$in).

Hold the timber firmly in a vice so it doesn't slip while being cut. Reposition as necessary so all cuts are made without compromising your safety. Use the jigsaw to cut around the outer shape of the handle, but not across the sloping end.

Use a chisel to shape the sloping end of the scraper. Keep the scraper firmly held in a vice and take extra care when using sharp tools. With a metal file or sanding sheet, round off the edges and sloping end, so the scraper is smooth in the hand.

Using the 8mm ($5/16$in) drill bit, make a hole at the top of the handle, which can be used to hang up the scraper. Attach a loop of strong string or a metal clip, if required, but don't make this out of anything that will snag when you put the tool in a pocket.

Use the dibber to make holes for large seeds, such as sunflowers, beans and pumpkins.

TIPS FOR USING THE SEED TRAYS

As well as filling them with compost to raise a wide selection of seedlings, you can also use the sturdy trays to move pots and produce around the garden.

Four plastic pots filled with different varieties of lettuce fit neatly into a tray.

- **Use linseed oil** or Danish oil to treat the tools and lend some degree of water resistance. Rub them down and re-treat every year or two.
- **Fill the large tray** with compost and use the tamper to firm this down to remove any air pockets. Water just enough to dampen the compost; any surplus will run through the gaps between slats in the base.
- **Sow leeks**, brassicas, tomatoes, and celery, thinly in trays filled with compost. When the seedlings are large enough, prick them out, pot them on and return the pots of young plants to the trays to grow on.
- **Sow large seeds**, such as pumpkins, beans and sunflowers, directly into 9cm (3½in) pots, or pot on 12 young plants into pots of this size and store in the larger tray.
- **Carry vulnerable plants** in the trays from the house to the greenhouse by day, and back again at night. This allows those who don't have any extra heat in the greenhouse to raise tender plants in early spring.
- **Trays are useful** as handy containers when harvesting vegetables.
- **Use the scraper** to remove earth that is stuck to the blade of a spade when digging heavy soil.
- **Mark sowing depths** along the length of the dibber to create a speedy aid when sowing seeds. Also take care not to leave an air pocket beneath the seed when you drop it in by firming soil gently around it.

OPPOSITE The tray is ideal for harvesting baby carrots and offers an easy way to carry tomato plants to the greenhouse.
RIGHT Potting on celery plants in a tray.

Slug-proof salad trays

You will need

For three trays 46cm x 34.5cm (18in x 14in)

- **Timber**
  - 6 x long sides: 46cm long, 95mm wide, and 17mm thick (18in x 3³/₄in x ³/₄in)
  - 6 x short sides: 31cm long, 95mm wide, and 17mm thick (12¹/₂in x 3³/₄in x ³/₄in)
  - 15 x base slats: 46cm long, 65mm wide, and 12mm thick (18in x 2¹/₂in x ¹/₂in)
  - 4 x legs for one box: 35cm long, 30mm wide, and 12mm thick (14in x 1¹/₄in x ¹/₂in)
- **Copper pipe** 19mm (³/₄in) external diameter 4 x 35cm (14in) for legs of one box
- **Rigid water pipe** 29mm (1¹/₄in) external diameter 4 x 35cm (14in) for legs for one box
- **Stainless steel screws**
  - 40 x 4mm x 50mm (No 8 x 2in)
  - 8 x 4mm x 70mm (No 8 x 2³/₄in)

- **Galvanised clout nails** 60 x 30mm (1¹/₄in)
- **4 jam jars**
- **4 small rubber boots**
- **Polythene and compost** for filling

TOOLS

- Tape measure
- Saw
- Hacksaw
- File
- Square
- Drill with 4mm (⁵/₃₂in) and 2mm (⁵/₆₄in) drill bits
- Countersink bit
- Screwdriver
- Hammer
- Pencil
- Sanding sheet and block
- Paper or card

This project shows three ways to protect salad crops from slugs and snails. You can make several trays using just one design, or try a range of options. Each system works well for growing slug-free salad, but copper legs are our favourite.

Slugs and snails are a nuisance in many gardens. They come out after dark and can dispatch seedlings in seconds or munch holes in the tastiest salad leaves. This may not matter much if you have a large plot and can afford to share the crops, but if you have a small backyard with just a few containers, it can be devastating.

This set us thinking. There are plenty of physical barriers that can deter slugs, so why not incorporate some of these options into three specially constructed growing boxes? Copper is a known barrier that slugs hate to cross; a boot full of sharp grit would be another deterrent; and we know these pests can't swim. Using these ideas we designed three sets of legs to work in different ways. The resulting trays have become one of our favourite projects, and have allowed us to grow lots of delicious salad leaves completely free of slug and snail damage.

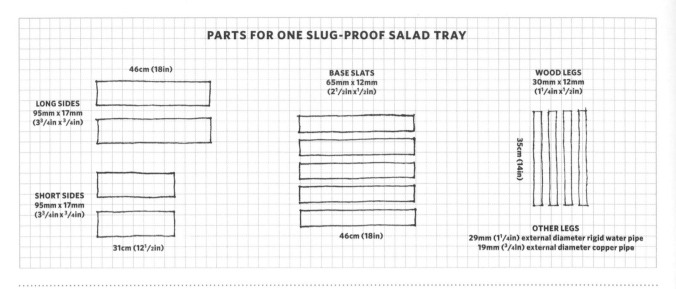

PARTS FOR ONE SLUG-PROOF SALAD TRAY

LONG SIDES
95mm x 17mm
(3³/₄in x ³/₄in)

46cm (18in)

SHORT SIDES
95mm x 17mm
(3³/₄in x ³/₄in)

31cm (12¹/₂in)

BASE SLATS
65mm x 12mm
(2¹/₂in x ¹/₂in)

46cm (18in)

WOOD LEGS
30mm x 12mm
(1¹/₄in x ¹/₂in)

35cm (14in)

OTHER LEGS
29mm (1¹/₄in) external diameter rigid water pipe
19mm (³/₄in) external diameter copper pipe

Making three salad trays

STEP 1 CUT COMPONENTS TO LENGTH

Use the tape measure, square and pencil to mark the timber and saw to length. A wood saw will cut through the water pipe. Use a hacksaw to cut through copper pipe (or ask a plumber to do this job for you). Make sure cut edges are straight and level.

STEP 2 SMOOTH THE EDGES

Smooth the cut surfaces of pipe with a file to remove sharp edges. This job is easier if the pipe is held in a clamp or workbench and you use the file with both hands (as shown). Use the sanding sheet and block to smooth any rough timber edges.

STEP 3 MAKE A MARKING TEMPLATE

Cut paper or card 95mm (3³/₄in) wide and make a folding line 9mm (³/₈in) from one end. Mark four points across this end: two 25mm (1in) from each side and two 15mm (⁵/₈in) from each side. Use to mark drilling points at each end of the long sides.

STEP 4 DRILL HOLES

Drill all points marked in Step 3. Using the 4mm (⁵/₃₂in) bit, make clearance holes at points marked 25mm (1in) from the sides and finish these with a countersink bit. Use the 2mm (⁵/₆₄in) bit to make pilot holes at the points 15mm (⁵/₈in) from the sides.

STEP 5 ASSEMBLE THE SIDES

Assemble the sides using 4mm x 50mm (No 8 x 2in) screws. Screw through the 4mm (⁵/₃₂in) holes drilled in Step 4, into the end-grain of the short sides to make a rectangle. Ensure all edges are flush and straight. Repeat to make all three frames.

STEP 6 FIT BASE SLATS

Make pilot holes 9mm (³/₈in) from each end of the base slats with the 2mm (⁵/₆₄in) drill bit. Use clout nails and hammer to fix the two outer slats. Space the other slats evenly across the base, and include small gaps for drainage. Repeat for all frames.

STEP 7 MARK DRILLING POINTS ON THE LEGS

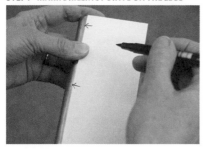

Mark two drilling points 10mm (³/₈in) and 75mm (3in) from one end of each leg. Mark the wooden legs off centre, 9mm (³/₈in) from one side. Centre the drilling points in both types of pipe. Use a marking template to line up pipe drilling points (as shown).

STEP 8 PREPARE COPPER PIPE FOR DRILLING

Hold the pipe firmly in a workbench or a vice and use a hammer and nail to punch a depression into the copper pipe before drilling. Make this deep enough to help locate the tip of the drill bit and to stop the bit from skidding around.

STEP 9 DRILL HOLES IN LEGS

Use the 4mm (⁵/₃₂in) bit to drill holes in all legs at the marked points. Drill right through both sides of pipe, keeping the drill as straight as possible. File any rough edges. Paint the trays before the legs are fitted, or use a preservative wood stain.

STEP 10 FIT LEGS ONTO TRAYS

Fix four copper legs to one box with 4mm x 50mm (No 8 x 2in) screws. Use 4mm x 70mm (No 8 x 2³/₄in) screws to fix four water pipe legs to a second box, and use 4mm x 50mm (No 8 x 2in) screws to fix four wooden legs to the third box.

STEP 11 LINE THE TRAYS

You can fill the trays with compost as they are. Or to prevent finer material falling between the gaps, line the boxes with polythene and puncture holes along the gaps in the base before filling. This keeps compost moist and protects the timber.

STEP 12 SET UP THE BOXES

Push copper legs into the ground or stand them directly on a hard surface. Place one jam jar under each water-pipe leg and fill with water. Wooden legs slip into a child's rubber boots; stand these in a tray of water or fill them with a slug repellent material.

SOWING AND GROWING TIPS FOR THE SALAD TRAYS

After filling with compost, either sow salad leaves directly into each tray or transplant small plants into them. You can plant closely, provided you pick leaves regularly while they are young.

Children love this fun salad tray and it's a great way to recycle their old boots.

- **Rocket, mizuna, lettuce,** mustard greens, pak choi, spinach, purslane, corn salad or cress will all grow well in the trays. You can also buy salad leaf mixes that contain some of these leaves.
- **Use good quality** seed compost and sow directly over the surface. Cover seed with 3mm (1/8in) compost. You can sow quite thickly (at around three pinches of seed per box) since the idea is to pick often while leaves are small. Buying in small plants will speed things up a little, but either way you should have leaves to pick within a few weeks.
- **Basil and coriander** both do well in the trays but they are best suited to lots of small plants rather than large specimens.
- **Make sure** the pipe doesn't touch the side of a jar and that leaves and trays don't touch anything that will create a bridge for slugs to climb up.
- **When one crop** is finished, remove all the plants and sow more seed. The compost may be exhausted after this first harvest, so either replace all, or some, of it. You can also use liquid feeds while crops are growing to top up the compost's nutrients.
- **An alternative idea** is to fit these various leg options to a selection of wooden crates, which are sometimes free from vegetable shops, or you can buy sturdy crates from DIY shops and garden centres.

OPPOSITE AND ABOVE Pristine young plants develop unhindered by slugs, creating a bountiful harvest.

Fitting out a garden shed

A garden shed is often an empty shell where tools and equipment are piled into corners along with garden produce. So make the most of this useful space by fitting it out with a workbench, shelves, a secure floor and racks for tools.

A new shed is a wonderful thing and offers a great storage space for tools and plants. Keep it tidy and well-organised by following the 12 easy steps overleaf and you will never again have to spend hours hunting for a sharpening stone or a trowel buried under a pile of pots.

Each tool hangs in a place of its own; just reach out a hand to take it down and you will know exactly where to put it back when you have finished. A workbench is great for sowing and potting up your plants, and shelves make good use of the vertical space. Add some bins and strong hooks, reinforce the floor and block any gaps, and you will double the shed's usefulness.

You may have to alter some dimensions to fit your particular shed but the techniques shown here will remain the same.

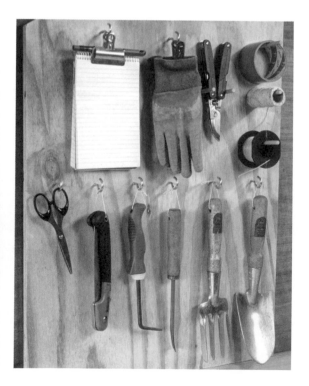

You will need

For a shed measuring 244cm x 244cm (96in x 96in)

FOR THE FLOOR
- **Small mesh galvanised fencing wire**
- **2 x pieces of hardboard:** 244cm long, 122cm wide (96in x 48in) or 4mm (1/4in) plywood sheets
- **Staples**
- **Galvanised nails** 20mm (3/4in)

FOR A 220CM X 60CM (87IN X 24IN) WORKBENCH
- **Timber**
  - 1 x backboard: 220cm long, 15cm wide, and 35mm thick (87in x 6in x 1½in)
  - 2 x middle and front boards: 220cm long, 22cm wide, and 35mm thick (87in x 9in x 1½in)
  - 3 x horizontal supports: 73cm long, 50mm wide, and 25mm thick (29in x 2in x 1in)
  - 1 x leg: 94cm long, 65mm wide, and 35mm thick (37in x 2½in x 1½in)
- **Screws** 4mm x 50mm (No 8 x 2in)

FOR A 220CM X 22CM (87IN X 9IN) SHELF
- **Timber**
  - 1 x shelf: 220cm x 22cm x 20mm (87in x 9in x 3/4in)
  - 3 x brackets: 18cm x 15cm x 20mm (7in x 6in x 3/4in)
- **Screws** 4mm x 40mm (No 8 x 1½in)

FOR A PEGBOARD FOR SMALL TOOLS
- **Plywood or MDF** 12mm (1/2in) thick
- **Wooden dowel** 6mm (1/4in) diameter
- **Small hooks**
- **Wood glue**
- **Screws** 4mm x 25mm (No 8 x 1in)

FOR A PEG RACK FOR LARGE TOOLS
- **Timber** 80cm x 50mm x 25mm (31½in x 2in x 1in)
- **Wooden dowel** 10mm (3/8in) diameter
- **Wood glue**
- **Screws** 4mm x 70mm (No 8 x 2¾in)

FOR TWO 75CM X 23CM (29½IN X 9IN) HANGING SHELVES
- **Timber** 2 x 75cm long, 23cm wide, 25mm thick (29½in x 9in x 1in)
- **Large hooks**
- **Rope**

TOOLS
- Drill with 4mm (5/32in), 10mm (3/8in), and 6mm (1/4in) drill bits
- Saw (preferably a jigsaw)
- Hammer
- Screwdriver
- Spirit level
- Tape measure
- Staple gun

PARTS FOR FITTING OUT A SHED

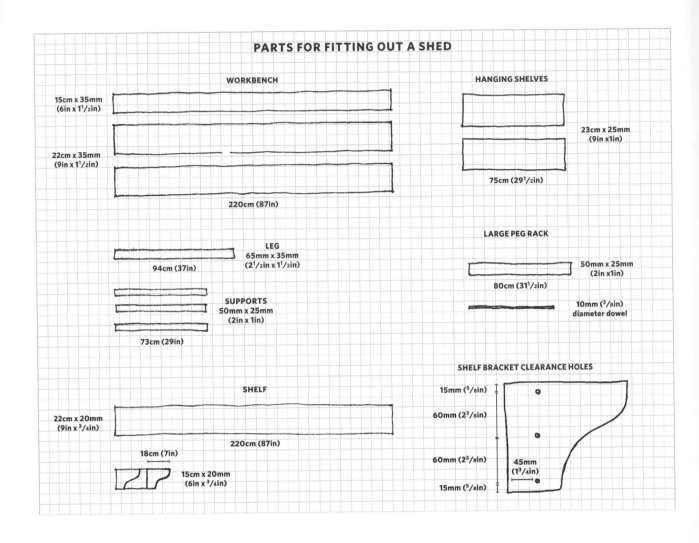

WORKBENCH

15cm x 35mm
(6in x 1¹/₂in)

22cm x 35mm
(9in x 1¹/₂in)

220cm (87in)

LEG
65mm x 35mm
(2¹/₂in x 1¹/₂in)
94cm (37in)

SUPPORTS
50mm x 25mm
(2in x 1in)
73cm (29in)

SHELF

22cm x 20mm
(9in x ³/₄in)
220cm (87in)

18cm (7in)

15cm x 20mm
(6in x ³/₄in)

HANGING SHELVES

23cm x 25mm
(9in x1in)

75cm (29¹/₂in)

LARGE PEG RACK

50mm x 25mm
(2in x1in)
80cm (31¹/₂in)

10mm (³/₈in)
diameter dowel

SHELF BRACKET CLEARANCE HOLES

15mm (⁵/₈in)

60mm (2³/₈in)

60mm (2³/₈in)   45mm
(1³/₄in)

15mm (⁵/₈in)

Fitting out the garden shed

STEP 1   ASSESS WHAT YOU HAVE GOT

Some new sheds have a more substantial timber framework or thicker boards on the walls than others. The framework is usually strong enough to use as a support, but if the boards are too thin to fix screws into, add extra pieces of timber. Also consider a polythene membrane to weatherproof it.

STEP 2   REINFORCE THE FLOOR

Staple galvanised fencing wire over the floor to keep out rodents. You can lay a double layer to create a smaller mesh size if necessary. Nail a layer of hardboard, or thin plywood over the top. Treat hardboard first by brushing down with water, then leave overnight before nailing in place.

STEP 3   CUT NOTCHES IN SHELF AND WORKBENCH

Measure and mark where these timbers will butt against the uprights of the frame. Cut out notches to the width and thickness of the uprights so the timber slots around the frame and sits flush against the wall with no gap. NOTE: a narrow board for the back of the workbench will be easier to handle.

STEP 4   FIT THE WORKBENCH

With 4mm (⁵/₃₂in) bit and three 4mm x 50mm (No 8 x 2in) screws, fit horizontal supports against the shed framework at each end. Fix the third support to the frame and the leg at the centre of the bench. Push the narrow board in place; set the other two boards on the supports to make a flat top.

STEP 5   CUT SHELF BRACKETS

Use a jigsaw to cut curved brackets. Draw around a cardboard template so each bracket is the same. Use the 4mm (⁵/₃₂in) bit to drill three clearance holes, evenly spaced and 45mm (1³/₄in) from the 15cm (6in) side of each bracket. This allows a strong fixing into the shed frame.

STEP 6   FIT THE SHELF

Determine the height of the shelf, taking into account the slope of the roof. Measure and mark these points. Use the 4mm x 40mm (No 8 x 1½in) screws to fix through the holes in the sides of the brackets and into the sides of the frame uprights. Ensure all bracket tops are level.

STEP 7   MAKE A PEGBOARD FOR SMALL TOOLS

Lay tools on the board and decide where to position them, then drill pilot holes and fix hooks directly into the board. Also drill 6mm (¹/₄in) holes for dowel pegs. Cut dowel to the length required and apply a little wood glue to one end. Tap the dowel into the drilled hole with a hammer.

STEP 8   FIT THE PEGBOARD

Use a 4mm (⁵/₃₂in) bit and 4mm x 25mm (No 8 x 1in) screws to fix the board directly onto the wall, or onto the frame if the walls aren't strong enough. You can draw around each tool with a thick marker so they are always returned to their correct place on the pegboard.

STEP 9   FIX STRONG HOOKS INTO ROOF SUPPORT

Screw extra lengths of 50mm x 25mm (2in x 1in) timber onto the roof frame, if needed, to create fixing points for hooks. Drill a hole slightly smaller than the thread of the hook and screw it in. Slip a screwdriver through the head of the hook and use for extra leverage to tighten it.

STEP 10   FIT THE PEG RACK

Lay tools out, mark both sides of each of the handles, drill 10mm (³/₈in) holes, glue and knock in 10mm (³/₈in) diameter dowels (as in Step 7). Position the rack, then drill and fit it: use two 4mm x 70mm (No 8 x 2³/₄in) screws through the frame uprights and into the grain at each end of the rack.

STEP 11   ASSEMBLE HANGING SHELVES

Use a 6mm (¹/₄in) drill bit to make a hole in each corner of each shelf. Loop the rope underneath, and pass the ends up through the holes at each end, so the bottom shelf is supported. Tie knots, large enough not to pull through the holes, and thread on the upper shelf.

STEP 12   FIT HANGING SHELVES

Check the knots to make sure the two shelves are parallel and at a good distance apart. Tie the loose ends of rope together at each end to make two hanging points: the knots must not slip under pressure. Adjust the lengths of rope to ensure the shelf unit is level, and hang on hooks.

TIPS FOR FITTING AND USING THE GARDEN SHED

If you have followed some, or all, of the steps, you will be surprised at just how much you can squeeze into your shed, and how easy it is to find what you need.

- **Sheds** come in different sizes and the timber used for construction is often different sizes too. This makes it difficult to give precise screw sizes, drill bits, lengths of timbers used, and so on. A certain amount is down to you to work out, once the basic instructions are understood. Make sure screws are long enough to go deep into the timbers, without punching through on the other side, and they shouldn't pull out under normal use. Long lengths of timber are also less likely to bow if they are thick enough.

- **The height of the bench** should allow you to stand comfortably with hands at a natural height and no stress on the back or shoulders. The width is determined by the size of your shed. Two or three planks are easier to handle than one solid piece, just lay these side by side across the supports, leaving no gaps in between.

- **Vary the length** of dowel on the peg board and tool rack, according to what you want to hold: use longer dowels for balls of string, for example, and shorter ones to hold secateurs in place.

- **You can hang** all sorts of things on hooks. Try storing strings of onions, or pumpkins in nets. Stuff bags with garden netting, or crop cover, and hang these up on the hooks too.

- **Dustbins** are also useful. Put a row under the bench and keep one for compost, one for lime, one for spare plant pots, and one without a lid for storing carrots and beetroot in sawdust.

LEFT Storage bins fit underneath the bench.
OPPOSITE Ensure the height of the bench is right for you to work comfortably.

Hinged extra tool storage

DIFFICULTY LEVEL ➕➕➕➕➕➕➕➕➕

HOURS TO COMPLETE 🕒🕒🕒🕒🕒🕒🕒🕒🕒

You will need

For a 160cm x 83cm (63in x 32¹/₂in) board to fit between uprights 79.5cm (31¹/₂in) apart

- **Exterior shuttering plywood (CDX)**
  160cm x 83cm x 19mm
  (63in x 32¹/₂in x ³/₄in)
- **Timber**
  - 1 x hinged side upright: 160 cm x 80mm x 35mm (63in x 3in x 1¹/₂in)
  - 1 x for opening side upright: 160 cm x 60mm x 35mm (63in x 2¹/₂in x 1¹/₂in)
  - 12mm (¹/₂in) dowel
- **Fittings**
  - 2 x strong galvanised T-hinges
  - 2 x galvanised gutter bolts (with nut and washer)
- **Stainless steel screws**
  - 4mm x 20mm (No 8 x ³/₄in)
  - 5mm x 100mm (No 10 x 4in)
- **Hooks**
- **Wood glue**

TOOLS

- Jigsaw
- Straight-edge
- Tape measure
- Hammer
- Square
- Saw
- Drill with 3mm (¹/₈in) and 12mm (¹/₂in) drill bits
- Screwdriver
- Pencil
- Mirror
- Masking tape
- Sanding sheet

If you have just one shed and too many tools to squeeze into it, try this simple idea. We have simply fitted an extra hinged door onto the frame, and effectively trebled our tool storage space.

The average shed isn't very big. Generally, it will have a door at one end and possibly a bench along one side. Used to store tools and compost, pots, a mower and maybe a few strings of onions, it soon begins to feel cramped. In terms of wall space, there is usually one gable end to hang long-handled tools and maybe some space along one wall, but if you have lots of equipment this is rarely sufficient.

This project solves the problem and comprises a hinged board fixed over tools already hanging on the wall. Fitted out with hooks and pegs, it provides areas on both sides of the board for all your kit. It's a simple project, but extremely useful. You can also apply the same technique to other sections of your shed wall; just remember to leave plenty of clearance space for the open board.

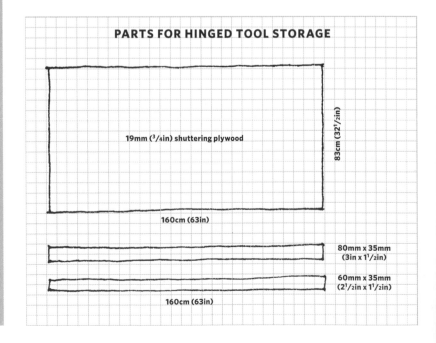

PARTS FOR HINGED TOOL STORAGE

19mm (³/₄in) shuttering plywood

83cm (32¹/₂in)

160cm (63in)

80mm x 35mm (3in x 1¹/₂in)

60mm x 35mm (2¹/₂in x 1¹/₂in)

160cm (63in)

Making the hinged extra tool storage

STEP 1 FIX UPRIGHTS OVER THE EXISTING FRAME

Using the 12mm (1/2in) bit, drill four holes 2cm (3/4in) deep in the hinged side upright and three in the opening side. Drill a 5mm (3/16in) hole into the base of each to allow 100mm (4in) screws to recess 2cm (3/4in) into the wood. Fix onto the shed frame.

STEP 2 CUT PLYWOOD TO SIZE

With a straight edge, mark a cutting line and follow this closely with the jigsaw to cut the plywood to size. One side of CDX ply is usually a higher grade than the other (which may have stamped markings),so choose the cleanest side as the outer face.

STEP 3 MARK FOR TOOL SUPPORTS

Arrange tools on the ply and mark where peg and hook supports will go. Dowels support large tools and hooks are for small ones. Repeat on other side of the board. The surface that will face the wall has a limited depth, so use it for flat-sided tools.

STEP 4 FIT A TOOL HOLDER (OPTIONAL)

You can also buy all sorts of tool holders. These often grip the handles of longer tools or you can hang smaller tools on them. They may not look as attractive as dowel pegs, but offer a quick way of fitting a holding device to the back of the board.

STEP 5 FIX ON THE HOOKS

Use the 3mm (1/8in) bit to drill holes at points marked for hooks. To avoid drilling all the way through the ply, add masking tape to show the depth you can safely drill to. Make sure hooks are fully screwed into place and are at 90 degrees to the board.

STEP 6 CUT THE DOWEL

Count how many dowel pegs you need: there are 21 on this tool rack. Using a mitre block will save time. Hold the dowel securely, so there is no threat to fingers, and cut 75mm (3in) lengths: these stick out of the board by 60mm (2 3/8in).

STEP 7 SAND EDGES

Roll the edges of the dowels around a piece of sanding sheet until they are smooth. Tools are less likely to slide off the pegs if the dowels are tilted slightly upwards. In order to get an even tilt on all pegs, follow the trick shown in Step 8.

STEP 8 A SIMPLE TRICK

Tape across the mirror at the angle you wish the pegs to sit in the board. Use the 12mm (1/2in) bit to drill holes and line the bit up with the angle of the tape across the mirror. You can ask a friend to help eye it up while you drill.

STEP 9 FIT THE DOWELS

Spread a thin layer of wood glue at the end of each dowel. Knock the dowels into the holes drilled in Step 8, so they sit at the same depth and angle. If they are a tight fit, you don't need to use glue, but if they are loose, glue is essential.

STEP 10 ADD ELASTIC BANDS

If you think the tools will slide off the dowels when the rack is opened and closed, wind elastic bands around the end of each peg. The bands provide enough friction to stop tools sliding forward. Try a colour system to mark which tool goes where.

STEP 11 FIT THE HINGES

Mount the hinges square to the edge of the board. Use 4mm x 20mm (No 8 x ³/₄in) screws, if those supplied are likely to punch through the board. Also fit one gutter bolt per hinge to give extra strength to support the weight of the tool-laden rack.

STEP 12 FIX THE BOARD IN PLACE

Find a support at the right height and stand the rack on it so both hands are free. Leave a 2mm (⁵/₆₄in) gap to ensure the 'door' doesn't bind (stick the edge of the square in next to the hinged edge of the board). Screw hinges to the hinged side upright.

TIPS FOR INSTALLING AND ADAPTING THE TOOL STORAGE

Both sides of this versatile rack can support a large number of tools, plus you have the original wall. And each tool has its place, helping you to keep the shed tidy.

Remember to allow clearance space at the bottom of the door.

- **The rack should close** smoothly against the opening side upright. Fit a magnetic catch, or a more secure lock, to keep tools stored safely.
- **Position the board** at a height that suits you, but take care that it doesn't bang into the pitched roof when you open it. The bottom edge works well at 30cm (12in) above the floor: this allows for some clearance over the top of any small items underneath.
- **Try a mock-up** if you can't picture the size of rack you will need. Lay tools out on a table, sheets of paper, or any other flat surface. See what fits where, and how much area is covered. Then cut a piece of card to this size and see how well it fits in your shed: this will save you from making something too small for the tools, or too big to fit the space.
- **Add an extra timber** to the frame uprights if you want a wider space between the hinged door and the wall to store more bulky tools on the inner side. Or simply use thicker uprights.
- **It's amazing** how many tools will fit onto a small wall space, and we find the greatest benefit is being able to locate everything we need easily. You can, of course, adjust and move things around as you acquire new tools or make a smaller door for another section of the shed.
- **Keep tools clean** and always return them to their given place.

Covered hotbed

Using manure to raise the soil temperature, a hotbed provides a warm growing environment for tender plants. Add a cover and the extra heat is contained, making it possible to start tomatoes, peppers, cucumbers, aubergines (eggplants) and melons earlier in the year.

Making a hotbed isn't a new idea. These structures have been used for centuries to give a little extra heat and to extend the growing season. Some large kitchen gardens have rows of traditional handcrafted timber and glass frames, which look lovely but can take considerable time, skill, and money to make.

This project is a modern take on the traditional hotbed. It has a strong wooden frame part-filled with fresh manure and covered with a layer of compost: the manure generates heat as it breaks down. The cover is light, tough and easy to work with; its insulating properties retain the heat, so plants benefit from the higher temperatures, and it folds away flat when not in use. This system also looks good and is very efficient. You can make it in a weekend and it should provide many years of extended growing seasons.

EXPERT TIP

Allow two days for this project so that the glue can dry overnight.

You will need

For a bed measuring 150cm x 50cm x 28cm (59in x 19³/₄in x 11in), with a cover 150cm x 49cm x 40cm (59in x 19¹/₄in x 16in)

- **Timber for bed**
  - 4 x decking boards for sides:
    150cm x 14cm x 32mm (59in x 5¹/₂in x 1¹/₄in)
  - 4 x decking boards for ends:
    43.5cm x 14cm x 32mm (17¹/₄in x 5¹/₂in x 1¹/₄in)
  - 6 x locater posts for bed:
    21cm x 45mm x 19mm (8¹/₄in x 1³/₄in x ³/₄in)
- **Timber for cover**
  - 2 x strips for lid:
    143cm x 19mm x 19mm (56in x ³/₄in x ³/₄in)
- **Clearwall polycarbonate sheet**
  4mm (⁵/₃₂in) with channel sections — order from online suppliers if not available locally.
  - 2 x sheets: 150cm x 105cm (59in x 41in), cut in Step 1, as shown in diagram on p.142
- **Screws (stainless steel or decking)**
  - 16 x 5mm x 80mm (No 10 x 3¹/₄in)
  - 12 x 4mm x 40mm (No 8 x 1¹/₂in)
  - 8 x 3.5mm x 20mm (No 6 x ³/₄in)
- **Evostick 007 grab and seal glue**, or equivalent
- **Cable ties** 3.6mm (¹/₈in)
- **Cleats and cord** (optional)

TOOLS

- Stanley knife
- Pliers
- Tape measure
- Marker pen
- Drill with 4mm (⁵/₃₂in) and 5mm (³/₁₆in) drill bits
- Screwdriver
- Glue gun
- Straight edge to cut against, such as a straight-cut piece of polycarbonate
- Clothes pegs

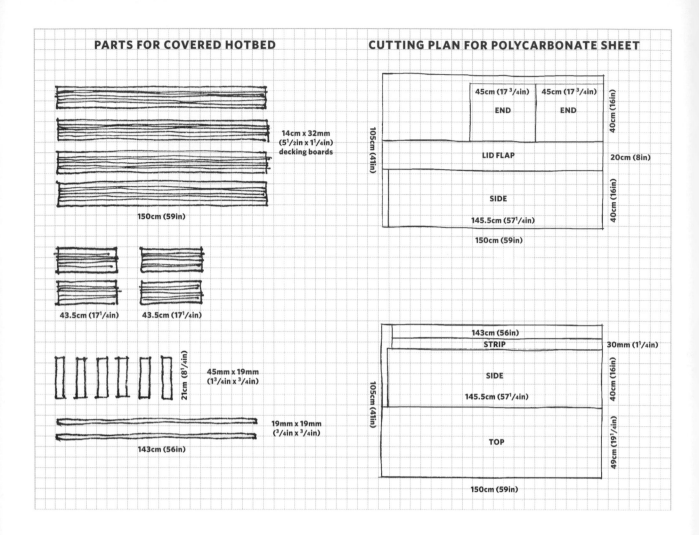

PARTS FOR COVERED HOTBED

14cm x 32mm
(5¹/₂in x 1¹/₄in)
decking boards

150cm (59in)

43.5cm (17¹/₄in)   43.5cm (17¹/₄in)

21cm (8¹/₄in)

45mm x 19mm
(1³/₄in x ³/₄in)

19mm x 19mm
(³/₄in x ³/₄in)

143cm (56in)

CUTTING PLAN FOR POLYCARBONATE SHEET

105cm (41in)

45cm (17³/₄in)   45cm (17³/₄in)
END   **END**
40cm (16in)

LID FLAP
20cm (8in)

SIDE
145.5cm (57¹/₄in)
40cm (16in)

150cm (59in)

105cm (41in)

143cm (56in)
STRIP
30mm (1¹/₄in)

SIDE
145.5cm (57¹/₄in)
40cm (16in)

TOP
49cm (19¹/₄in)

150cm (59in)

Making the covered hotbed

STEP 1 FOLLOW THE MARKING DIAGRAM

Using a straight edge, mark the polycarbonate sheet to the sizes shown above and cut out with a Stanley knife. The UV-protected side goes on the outside and usually has a protective covering. The channels should be set horizontally for the sides, so water doesn't run into the walls.

STEP 2 DRILL CLEARANCE HOLES

With a 5mm (³/₁₆in) bit, drill two clearance holes at each end of the 150cm (59in) lengths of decking. The holes should be 16mm (⁵/₈in) from the end of the decking boards and make them in the bottom of the outer grooves: this ensures the screw heads will be sunk below the surface.

STEP 3 ASSEMBLE THE TWO HOTBED FRAMES

Join together two sides and two ends per frame using 5mm x 80mm (No 10 x 3¹/₄in) screws. Screw through holes drilled in Step 2 and straight into the end-grain of the shorter pieces; you will not need to drill pilot holes into the grain. Make sure the corners are square and frames lie level.

STEP 4 FIT LOCATER POSTS IN ONE FRAME

With the 4mm (⁵/₃₂in) bit, drill two holes in each locater post, 60mm (2¹/₄in) from the top and 30mm (1¹/₄in) from the bottom. Using 4mm x 40mm (No 8 x 1¹/₂in) screws, fix these in the corners and midpoints of the frames, projecting 45mm (1³/₄in) above and 25mm (1in) below the sides.

STEP 5 DRILL FOUR EVENLY SPACED HOLES

Using a sharp steel or carbon 4mm (⁵/₃₂in) drill bit, make four evenly spaced holes in the polycarbonate sheet, 8mm (⁵/₁₆in) from edges of the 40cm (16in) sides and ends. Drill in the middle of a channel section. Use clothes pegs as clamps to drill through four layers at once.

STEP 6 JOIN EDGES WITH CABLE TIES

Fix cable ties through holes to join all four walls together (UV protected side facing outwards). Then drill seven holes along one long edge of the top and at the same spacing along the lid flap: drill behind the first channel in the polycarbonate. Use cable ties to join the top to the lid flap.

STEP 7 FIT TIMBER STRIPS ON TOP AND LID FLAP

Mark 20mm (³/₄in) from the edge and 35mm (1³/₈in) from each end of the non-hinged side of the top and the flap. Spread glue thinly on one side of the timber strips. Place the timber strips between the marks just made. Clamp until the glue sets, or fix with 3.5mm x 20mm (No 6 x ³/₄in) screws.

STEP 8 MAKE A GROOVE TO HOLD THE LID

Screw the strip of polycarbonate that measures 143cm (56in) onto the strip of timber on the lid flap. This should protrude by 6mm (¹/₄in) beyond the edge of the timber and towards the edge of the lid flap. The resulting groove cross section will hold the lid in place when it is raised.

STEP 9 ASSEMBLE THE BASE AND FILL

Put the wooden frame in place (top section fits snuggly over the bottom one) and fill the lower section with fresh, straw-based manure. Cover this with 10cm (4in) of compost. Fresh manure gets hot, so leave the heat to stabilise for a few days before planting up the bed.

STEP 10 PUT THE WALLS IN PLACE AND PLANT

Plant with melons, cucumbers, peppers, aubergines (eggplants), or any tender plant that needs some protection. Ensure the roots of small plants are in the compost, not the manure. Slide the polycarbonate walls over the wooden frame: the hinges should move easily and the cover fit snugly.

STEP 11 PUT THE LID ON

Peel the protective covering from the polycarbonate. The lid sits on top, with the strip of timber inside one wall. The flap will hang down at 90 degrees when the lid is closed. Tuck the strip of timber just behind a wall edge when the lid is raised. This keeps it braced and in position, as shown.

TIPS FOR GROWING CROPS IN THE COVERED HOTBED

The covered hotbed will aid the growth of many tender crops, but remember to keep it well ventilated as it can get too hot during the day for some plants.

Cucumbers will benefit from the extra heat afforded by the hotbed.

- **Choose a sheltered** sunny location for your hotbed, ideally close to a heat-retaining wall, if you intend to use it outdoors.
- **Line the base** with strong polythene to protect a tiled or wooden surface from the manure, but water carefully to prevent waterlogging if the moisture can't drain away.
- **Fit metal cleats** on an outdoor hotbed frame. Tie strong cord over the polycarbonate cover between the cleats, to stop it from blowing away.
- **Aubergines** (eggplants) and peppers grow very well in this system outdoors. During a hot summer, remove the cover and allow them to grow on; plants can be more productive in the hotbed than their siblings in the greenhouse.
- **Melons and cucumbers** really benefit from early planting in a covered hotbed placed in an unheated greenhouse. Always raise the lid or remove it altogether during the day: temperatures are already higher in a greenhouse, so plants may overheat and suffer from inadequate ventilation in a closed hotbed.
- **Remember to water** regularly when the hotbed is covered, but don't saturate the manure mix or it will not heat up.
- **Remove the top**, and leave the walls in place, when plants first outgrow the cover; plants can still benefit from extra protection from the walls.
- **Remove the walls** before the plants become too confined or congested, or removal of the walls becomes difficult.
- **The wooden frame** stays in place until all the plants are removed, at which point you can refill it and replant to get the most from the extended growing seasons the hotbed provides.

LEFT Remove the lid when plants start to grow above the height of the walls.

RIGHT You can increase your range of tender crops further by placing the hotbed inside a greenhouse or polytunnel.

Mini-greenhouse

A mini-greenhouse really extends the growing opportunities in a small garden and you will soon see the difference between outdoor tomatoes and those that are sheltered from the cold, wind and rain.

Many gardens aren't large enough for a full-sized greenhouse or polytunnel, and not every gardener can afford to buy these structures. But if you long for some under-cover growing space, then don't be deterred! It isn't difficult to make a mini-greenhouse that fits your space exactly. This simple structure is designed to work as a growing aid from spring to autumn. It isn't intended to support heavy snowfall, but the polythene is easy to remove during the winter. You can also

adapt the design to make a smaller structure, place it next to a fence or wall for additional shelter, or include more hoops or braces to cope with harsher weather. But whatever the design, we recommend using the strongest polythene you can afford.

Even a small structure opens up the possibility of growing tomatoes, peppers, or early strawberries, for example, and a greenhouse is invaluable for raising a whole range of vegetable plants from seed.

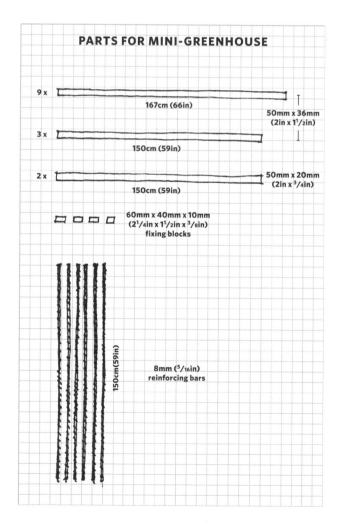

PARTS FOR MINI-GREENHOUSE

9 x — 167cm (66in) — 50mm x 36mm (2in x 1¹/₂in)

3 x — 150cm (59in) —

2 x — 150cm (59in) — 50mm x 20mm (2in x ³/₄in)

60mm x 40mm x 10mm (2¹/₄in x 1¹/₂in x ³/₈in) fixing blocks

150cm (59in) 8mm (⁵/₁₆in) reinforcing bars

You will need

For a structure measuring 167cm x 150cm (66in x 59in)

- **Timber (pressure-treated):**
  - 9 x side braces: 167cm x 50mm x 36mm (66in x 2in x 1¹/₂ in)
  - 3 x door, rail, and back pieces: 150cm x 50mm x 36mm (59in x 2in x 1¹/₂in)
  - 2 x 'sandwich' pieces: 150cm x 50mm x 20mm (59in x 2in x ³/₄in)
  - 4 x fixing blocks: 60mm x 40mm x 10mm (2¹/₄in x 1¹/₂in x ³/₈in)

- **Reinforcing bars**
  6 x 150cm x 8mm (59in x ⁵/₁₆in) as used to reinforce concrete

- **Semi-rigid water pipe (bendable)**
  - 3 x hoops: 435cm x 25mm (171in x 1in) external diameter
  - 1 x 30cm (12in x ³/₄in) to make ring clips to fit round the pipe

- **Heavy gauge polythene**
  - 500cm x 500cm (200in x 200in) for cover
  - 200cm x 200cm (80in x 80in) for door

- **Fittings**
  27 x galvanised pipe clips to fit around pipe

- **Screws (preferably stainless steel)**
  - 54 x 4mm x 20mm (No 8 x ³/₄in)
  - 16 x 4mm x 40mm (No 8 x 1¹/₂in)
  - 2 x 5mm x 70mm (No 10 x 2³/₄in)

TOOLS

- Hacksaw
- Wood saw
- Screwdriver
- Tape measure
- Pencil
- Hammer
- Sanding sheet
- Bradawl
- Spirit level (optional)

Making the mini-greenhouse

STEP 1   POSITION THE REINFORCING BARS

Knock three bars into the ground along each side of the proposed structure. Allow 80cm (32in) between each bar and knock them down until 110cm (43in) remains above soil level. Keep them vertical and check that the heights are all the same.

STEP 2   FIT THE PIPES

Slot the pipe over one piece of reinforcing rod, bend it round to make a smooth curve at the top, and slot it over the rod on the opposite side. Repeat to make three hoops. Push the pipe down until the curve on all three hoops is even and level.

STEP 3   MARK POINTS FOR PIPE CLIPS

Check that pipe clips grip the pipe firmly: give a squeeze to tighten them if needed. Place a pipe clip at each end and in the middle of seven of the 167cm (66in) lengths of timber. Mark where the fixing screws will go, and use a bradawl to punch holes.

STEP 4   FIT ONE SIDE BRACE

Hold a 167cm (66in) timber along one side of the frame, 20cm (8in) above the ground. Fit pipe clips round the pipe where marked. With 4mm x 20mm (No 8 x ¾in) screws, fix into the pre-punched holes. Ensure the timber is level and clips grip tightly.

STEP 5   FIT REMAINING SIDE BRACES

Use the pipe clips to fit all the lengths of timber, as in Step 4, to brace the structure. Aim for even spacing and fix one of these pieces of timber across the top of the hoops to form a ridge. You can add extra braces for greater strength, if required.

STEP 6   MAKE RING CLIPS

Use the hacksaw to cut ten 8mm (5/16in) rings from the 30cm (12in) pipe (used to fit the polythene). Cut a slit in each to make a split ring. Make sure there is enough flex for the ring to open, but enough tension for the ring to close and grip.

STEP 7   FIT THE POLYTHENE

Spread polythene over frame. Roll it around a 167cm (66in) timber on each side and fix at ground level with pipe clips. Fold the polythene at the front of the frame, and use 4mm x 40mm (No 8 x 1½in) screws to fix four fixing blocks to braces to secure it.

STEP 8   FIT THE RING CLIPS

Use the ring clips, made in Step 6, to tidy up the polythene around the sides of the door opening. Aim for a neat finish with no flapping ends and polythene tight across the frame. There is no need to use clips across the top part of the hoop.

STEP 9   FIT THE DOOR RAIL

Roll the top front edge of the polythene tightly around the 150cm (59in) rail piece of timber. Hold this level against the front of the frame. With 5mm x 70mm (No 10 x 2¾in) screws, fix into the ends of the top two side braces to make a door rail.

STEP 10 FIT THE BACK

Gather polythene neatly at the back of the frame and wrap twice around the 150cm (59in) back piece of timber. You can screw this onto a fence, or onto the wooden side of the raised bed to give more rigidity. Or sandwich between two lengths of timber and hold it down with weights.

STEP 11 MAKE THE DOOR

Cut polythene to cover the front opening with a 10cm (4in) overlap at each side. Roll and grip the lower edge between a door piece and a 'sandwich' piece. Use 4mm x 40mm (No 8 x 1½in) screws to fix these all together. Roll top edge of polythene around a sandwich piece so door fits the opening.

STEP 12 TIE DOOR CATCHES

Screw the rolled sandwich piece to the door rail; roll door down to close. You can make a fancier catch, but some strong twine works well to hold the door open. Roll the bottom up neatly so polythene doesn't sag. The door should hang well when shut; hold the sides closed with more ring clips.

TIPS FOR CONSTRUCTION AND GROWING IN THE MINI-GREENHOUSE

Add a board in the middle of the bed to make a narrow path and use the greenhouse for all types of tender crops and those that benefit from extra protection.

Strawberry plants will produce an early crop in a greenhouse.

- **You can alter the dimensions** to suit your garden. A narrow span is best in regions that experience high rainfall which could damage wider, unsupported areas of polythene. Make sure that the hoops are no more than 80cm (32in) apart and use pipe that is rigid enough not to distort.
- **We improved the design** when we started to use it, so make sure you follow the step-by-step guide, even if you spot some small differences in the photographs.
- **Designed for a sheltered** small garden, this structure will require weights, or fix the lower edges to a frame, if you want to use it in an area that is not as well protected.
- **Allow plenty of polythene** to roll onto the lower edge timbers and cut off excess when fitting to the frame. You can remove excess polythene, but if it's too short, you can't make it stretch.
- **Plant tomatoes directly** into enriched border soil. Choose varieties to suit the height of the frame you have made and nip out growing points when the plants reach the top. Don't plant too close and keep tomatoes well fed and watered for the best crops.
- **Strawberries do well** if grown in 20cm (8in) pots. You can move them out of the greenhouse if the weather improves, but they will benefit from early protection to give luscious late-spring fruits.
- **Use growing bags** for peppers and courgettes (zucchini). Move these outside when the weather improves to create more space for tomatoes. Movable pots help to maximise the potential of the growing space.

Copper-bottom cold frame

You will need

For a frame measuring 122cm x 60cm (48in x 24in)

- **Timber**
  - 4 x boards: 122cm x 22.5cm x 25mm (48in x 9in x 1in)
  - 4 x boards: 55cm x 22.5cm x 25mm (22in x 9in x 1in)
  - 2 x corner posts: 12.5cm x 50mm x 50mm (5in x 2in x 2in)
  - 2 x corner posts: 19cm x 50mm x 50mm (7¹/₂in x 2in x 2in)
  - 4 x corner posts: 24cm x 50mm x 50mm (9¹/₂in x 2in x 2in)
- **Catches**
  - 2 x 20cm x 20mm x 25mm (8in x ³/₄ x 1in)
  - 2 x 15cm x 20mm x 25mm (6in x ³/₄in x 1in)
- **Toughened glass or Perspex** 62cm x 122cm (25in x 48in)
- **Copper**
  - 360cm x 10cm (144in x 4in) or a 60cm x 60cm (24in x 24in) sheet to cut into strips
- **Stainless steel screws**
  - 46 x 5mm x 50mm (No 10 x 2in)
  - 4 x 5mm x 35mm (No 10 x 1³/₈in)
- **Sanding sheet** 80 grit and wooden block
- **Copper nails** 50mm (2in)

TOOLS

- Jigsaw or handsaw
- Drill
- 5mm (³/₁₆in) drill bit
- Screwdriver
- Pencil
- Ruler
- Tin-snips

Make this simple cold frame to help raise early semi-tender crops, or to tuck up overwintering seedlings and harden off young plants in spring. The copper bottom keeps plants healthy by warding off slugs and snails.

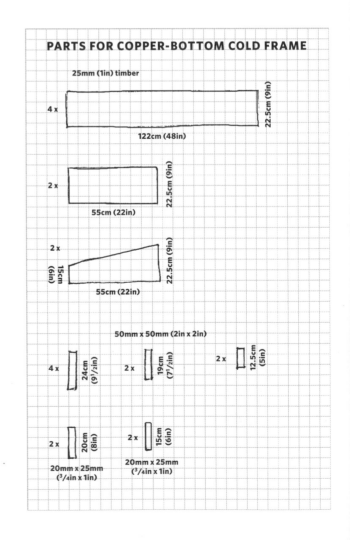

PARTS FOR COPPER-BOTTOM COLD FRAME

25mm (1in) timber

4 x — 122cm (48in) — 22.5cm (9in)

2 x — 55cm (22in) — 22.5cm (9in)

2 x — 15cm (6in) / 55cm (22in) — 22.5cm (9in)

50mm x 50mm (2in x 2in)

4 x — 24cm (9¹/₂in)

2 x — 19cm (7¹/₂in)

2 x — 12.5cm (5in)

2 x — 20cm (8in) — 20mm x 25mm (³/₄in x 1in)

2 x — 15cm (6in) — 20mm x 25mm (³/₄in x 1in)

Every kitchen garden should have a cold frame and while these structures aren't cheap to buy, they are relatively inexpensive to make.

The band of copper, as a slug defence, adds something really special, helping you to grow hole-free salad crops through the winter and protect small seedlings in spring when these pests are particularly destructive. With a bit of timely planting, it is possible to harvest potatoes, courgettes (zucchini) and strawberries in late spring. This cold frame should take less than a day to complete. The design shown is made in two layers, so plants can grow reasonably tall before they reach the cover, but you could make three layers for a deeper frame for taller plants.

The angled top, when positioned to face the sun, ensures the maximum light reaches your growing plants. Two turn-catches keep the lid in place when closed, while allowing you to raise it up for ventilation.

Making the cold frame

STEP 1 CUT OUT THE SLOPING SIDES

The slope on the top sides of this frame runs from 22.5cm to 15cm (9in to 6in). Mark the 15cm (6in) point at one end of two 55cm x 22.5cm (22in x 9in) timber boards. Draw a line and saw between these points. Sand all rough edges.

STEP 2 DRILL CLEARANCE HOLES

Using a 5mm ($^3/_{16}$in) drill bit, drill three, evenly spaced clearance holes 50mm (2in) from the ends of the long boards and 25mm (1in) from the ends of the short boards. Make just two holes on the 15cm (6in) end of the sloping boards (see Step 1).

STEP 3 ASSEMBLE THE LOWER FRAME

Support the corners as you screw the sides onto the 24cm (9½in) corner posts. The posts should stick up 2cm (¾in) above the sides to allow the top layer of the frame to slot over them. The 122cm (48in) pieces overlap the ends of the 55cm (22in) pieces.

STEP 4 FIT CORNER POSTS ON SLOPING SIDES

Fit corner posts at each end of the sloping sides (mirror images). Fix the 12.5cm (5in) posts to the 15cm (6in) end and the 19cm (7½in) posts to the 22.5cm (9in) end. The posts must allow the top to slot onto the lower frame, and glass lid to lie flat on top.

STEP 5 ASSEMBLE THE TOP SECTION

Assemble the top section of the frame, adjusting if necessary to create a good fit between the two sections. Ensure that both frames are square and that the top edge isn't twisted. Lower posts should fit snugly into the top frame without forcing.

STEP 6 SMOOTH THE GLASS

If the glass has unpolished edges, you can use the sanding sheet, wrapped around a wooden block, to smooth it. It is safest to do this outdoors and wear a mask. Always follow safety precautions when working with glass and do not touch sharp edges.

STEP 7 MAKE TURN CATCHES

With two 35mm (1³/₈in) screws, join the 20cm (8in) and 15cm (6in) timber for each catch, creating a step at each end. Fix each catch in place with a 50mm (2in) screw, 5cm (2in) from its long end. Leave the screw loose so the catch can rotate.

STEP 8 ATTACH THE COPPER STRIP

Attach the copper strip with copper nails to the lower edge of the frame, with 50mm (2in) below the edge: this will be pushed into the soil when positioning the frame. Use tin-snips to cut strips 10cm (4in) wide if using copper sheet.

STEP 9 POSITION THE FRAME

Choose a sunny spot for your frame. Push the copper down into the soil. Add some compost to the base and you are ready to get growing. If left untreated, the timber will darken with age. Remove the lid on hot days, or when plants outgrow the space.

SOWING AND GROWING TIPS FOR COLD FRAMES

A cold frame will not protect plants when air temperatures dip below freezing, but it is ideal for growing early crops of potatoes, strawberries, and courgettes.

Salad leaves are reasonably hardy and will survive in winter in a cold frame.

- **Salad leaves**, such as rocket, are sown direct in a 1cm (3/8in) deep drill in the cold frame compost. Sow from mid- to late summer for autumn crops, or from late summer to early autumn for winter crops.
- **Early potatoes** are planted from mid- to late winter. Push the tubers into the compost so they are covered to a depth of 15cm (6in). If it is very cold when the first leaves come through, cover with a layer of horticultural fleece, or crop cover, inside the frame.
- **A single courgette** (zucchini) or pumpkin grows well in this size of frame, but it is worth sowing three seeds if sowing direct. Cover seeds with 15mm (1/2in) compost and choose the strongest seedling to grow on if all three survive. Alternatively, buy a plant in spring and put it in glorious isolation in the middle of the frame. The plant will outgrow the frame, but by then the weather will be warm enough for the courgette plant to survive unprotected.
- **Early strawberries** crop well in 20cm (8in) pots filled with compost. You can move these into the frame when the winter salad is over. Move strawberry pots out to a corner of the garden when plants finish fruiting in late spring or early summer.
- **Young plants** can be hardened off in a cold frame, which works very well as a halfway house between a greenhouse and outdoor beds. Hardening off acclimatises early spring plantings such as leeks, beetroot, beans, sweet peas and bedding plants to colder conditions. To do this, simply place the seedlings in the cold frame a few weeks before the last frosts and keep the lid on day and night for a couple of days. Then open the lid during the day, closing it again at night, for another week or two. Plant seedlings outside when all risk of frost has passed.

Grow courgettes (zucchini) in a cold frame for early crops.

You will get an early crop of potatoes from a mid-winter planting.

Apple storage trays

Apples will keep for months in a cool dry place, especially if you stack them in storage racks that separate the fruits and allow air to circulate. These practical racks also pack a lot of apples into a small space in a shed or garage.

An apple tree laden with fruit is one of the most beautiful sights of autumn. It's also a delight to pick the fruit to make jams or chutneys and to fill the freezer with pies, puddings and sauce. These are all great ways to use windfalls, but what if you want to eat the fresh fruit for as long as possible or keep it in good condition until you have time to make all the goodies to fill the freezer and storage jars?

The answer is to put the apples into store. Lots of varieties, and especially cookers, will keep for months if you store them well. This can be as simple as spreading fruit out across a dry cellar floor, but an even better way is to make some specially designed apple storage racks. Make as many as you need and stack them on a bench or on the floor.

You can also use the racks to store pears for a few weeks.

You will need

For a single tray measuring 50cm x 45cm (20in x 17¹/₂in)

- **Timber**

(Multiply by four for four stacking trays)

- 2 x back and front: 50cm x 95mm x 19mm (20in x 3³/₄in x ³/₄in)
- 2 x sides: 40.8cm x 95mm x 19mm (16in x 3³/₄in x ³/₄in)
- 4 x slats: 50cm x 44mm x 19mm (20in x 1³/₄in x ³/₄in)
- 2 x outer slats: 42cm x 44mm x 19mm (16¹/₂in x 1³/₄in x ³/₄in)
- 4 x corner posts: 12cm x 44mm x 19mm (4³/₄in x 1³/₄in x ³/₄in)
- 4 x spacers: 40.8cm x 19mm x 19mm (16in x ³/₄in x ³/₄in)

- **Screws**
- 18 x 4mm x 40mm (No 8 x 1¹/₂in) self-piloting
- 16 x 4mm x 30mm (No 8 x 1¹/₄in) self-piloting

TOOLS

- Saw
- Drill with 5mm (³/₁₆in) drill bit
- Countersink bit
- Screwdriver
- Square
- Hammer
- Pencil
- Tape measure
- Sanding sheet
- Hand plane

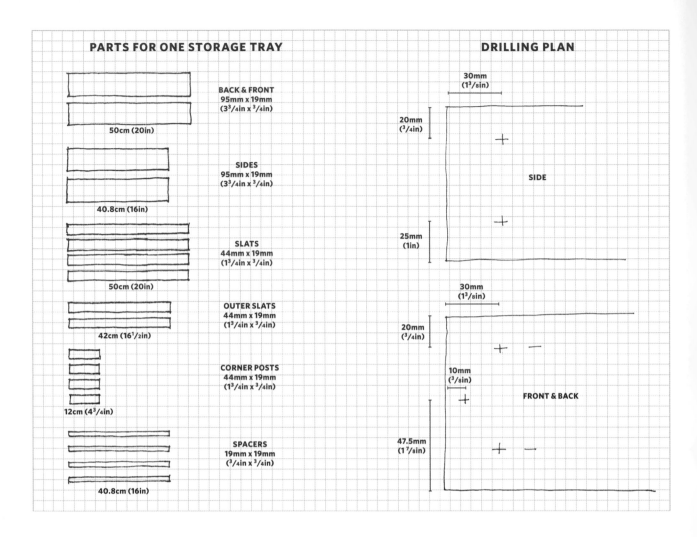

PARTS FOR ONE STORAGE TRAY

BACK & FRONT
95mm x 19mm
(3³/₄in x ³/₄in)
50cm (20in)

SIDES
95mm x 19mm
(3³/₄in x ³/₄in)
40.8cm (16in)

SLATS
44mm x 19mm
(1³/₄in x ³/₄in)
50cm (20in)

OUTER SLATS
44mm x 19mm
(1³/₄in x ³/₄in)
42cm (16¹/₂in)

CORNER POSTS
44mm x 19mm
(1³/₄in x ³/₄in)
12cm (4³/₄in)

SPACERS
19mm x 19mm
(³/₄in x ³/₄in)
40.8cm (16in)

DRILLING PLAN

30mm
(1³/₈in)

20mm
(³/₄in)

SIDE

25mm
(1in)

30mm
(1³/₈in)

20mm
(³/₄in)

10mm
(³/₈in)

FRONT & BACK

47.5mm
(1⁷/₈in)

Making the apple storage trays

STEP 1 MARK OUT AND CUT TIMBER TO SIZE

Use a square and pencil on the faces and edges of the timber, to mark it to length. Cut out the timber sizes listed, keeping edges as square and straight as possible. It is a good idea to sand any rough edges and remove splinters now, so all the wood is smooth to the touch and easy to handle.

STEP 2 MARK DRILLING POINTS

Mark all drilling points on the four sides of the frame, following the measurements on the drilling plan diagram above. The back and front will overlap the sides. Three drilling points are made on each end of the back and front, and two drilling points on each end of the sides.

STEP 3 ROUND CORNERS ON THE SLATS

Use a hand plane to chamfer the slats. This allows fruit to sit neatly in place. This stage can be accomplished much faster if you have the appropriate power tools (see p. 16). Alternatively, rub the slats with a sanding sheet to take off the sharp edges and corners so these don't bruise the fruit.

STEP 4 DRILL GUIDE HOLES

Use the drill and 5mm (³/₁₆ in) bit to make guide holes for the screws, and the countersink bit to neaten the edges of the drill holes and ensure the screw heads lie flush with the surface of the timber. Rub the holes with a sanding sheet before putting the frame together.

STEP 5 ASSEMBLE THE FRAME

Position each corner post 10mm (³/₈in) up from the bottom of the frame. Use the shorter screws to fix the sides, front and back to the corner posts; use longer screws to fix the front and back to the sides. Use the hammer to tap the frame into shape so the corners make right angles.

STEP 6 FIT THE SLATS

Space the slats evenly across the base of the frame. The shorter slats go at the outer edges, so frames can stack one on top of the other. Hammer the tip of the long screws in, so the slats don't move once in position, and screw down properly when everything is in the right place.

STEP 7 FIT THE SPACERS

The 19mm x 19mm (³/₄in x ³/₄in) spacers prevent the fruits from touching. Measure your tray before you cut the spacers to length. Cut them to approximately 2mm (⁵/₆₄in) less than the internal measurement of the tray from front to back. They should slot in easily but stay in place.

STEP 8 STACK THE TRAYS

Make all the trays in the same way, and stack them on top of each other to create a neat storage system. The corner posts of each tray will fit into the slot in the tray above: reduce the outer edges of the protruding posts with a plane if needed. Trays should lift on and off with ease.

You can make any number of trays, depending on how much fruit you need to store. They form a sturdy tower but if you want to stack more than six or seven trays, set them against a wall to prevent them toppling over. Also stack the apples that have the shortest storage life on top.

TIPS FOR USING THE APPLE STORAGE TRAYS

Make as many trays as you need and stack them up to store your fruit. You can make larger trays, but remember that they will be heavier to lift when full of fruit.

- **Change the height** of the top tray to fit the space if the storage rack is to be used where height is restricted. There is no problem if sides aren't quite so deep for the top tray and there is no need for protruding corner posts either. Of course, the system is more flexible if the trays are identical and hence will fit in any order in the stack.
- **Only store disease-free** and unblemished fruit, and place the racks in a cool, dry place where the apples will keep for longer.
- **Light doesn't harm** stored apples, but warmth from the sun streaming in at a window isn't ideal. Black out windows on sheds used for storage, or move the racks to a dark corner.
- **You can wrap** each apple in newspaper before putting it in the rack: this helps to reduce the spread of moulds and rot, but it also makes it more difficult to check stored fruit without unwrapping each one.
- **Sort different varieties** of apple into separate trays. Put those that keep the longest in the bottom tray and those you plan to use first at the top: work your way down to minimise losses.
- **Check trays** every few weeks and remove any rotten or damaged fruit.
- **Apples aren't the only thing!** Fill some trays with pears, some with garlic or onions, and others with small pumpkins and squash.

Check windfalls and picked fruits are blemish-free before storing.

You can wrap each apple to reduce the spread of rot.

Carrot fly cover

You will need

**For a carrot fly cover measuring
366cm x 122cm x 31cm (144in x 48in x 12in)**

- **Timber**
  50mm x 25mm (2in x 1in) pressure-treated

  For the top of the frame:
  - 2 x 366cm (144in)
  - 5 x 112cm (44in)

  For the two side frames:
  - 4 x 366cm (144in)
  - 10 x 21cm (8in)

  For the two end frames:
  - 4 x 117cm (46in)
  - 6 x 21cm (8in)

- **Fixings**
  - 3 x brass or galvanised hinges with screws
  - 3 x cleats with screws
  - Small fencing staples

- **Stainless steel screws**
  - 84 x 5mm x 100mm (No 10 x 4in)
  - 8 x 5mm x 60mm (No 10 x 2³/₈in)
  - 18 x 4mm x 40mm (No 8 x 1¹/₂in)

- **Insect-proof netting (very fine mesh)**
  500cm x 225cm (198in x 90in) for this cover

- **Rope or washing line**
  3 x 66cm (26in) lengths

- **Gasket**
  Foam, rubber, underlay, or extra netting

TOOLS

- Drill with 4mm (⁵/₃₂in) and 5mm (³/₁₆in) drill bits
- Saw and hammer
- Square
- Staple gun and staples
- Scissors
- Tape measure
- Clamp
- Plane, or sanding sheet and block
- Card and pencil

This protective frame fits snugly over a raised bed and it's fairly easy to make. Guarding roots against carrot fly, it can also prevent butterflies, birds and frost damaging your crops.

Carrot flies are attracted by the scent of the plants' foliage and they will fly for miles, or squeeze through the smallest gaps, in order to lay eggs near the roots. A batch of newly-hatched grubs can then riddle your crops with tunnels.

Some gardeners put up a barrier and leave the top open when growing carrots. This can work because the female fly stays close to the ground after she has mated, looking for a place to lay eggs. However, the flies go high up in the air to mate and it is only after the female has dropped down to ground level that her flight is limited in this way. If females fall into the middle of a carrot bed, then an open barrier is no use at all and the flies can lay eggs among the young carrot plants.

This protective cover is a more secure and efficient way to keep these pests off your carrot patch.

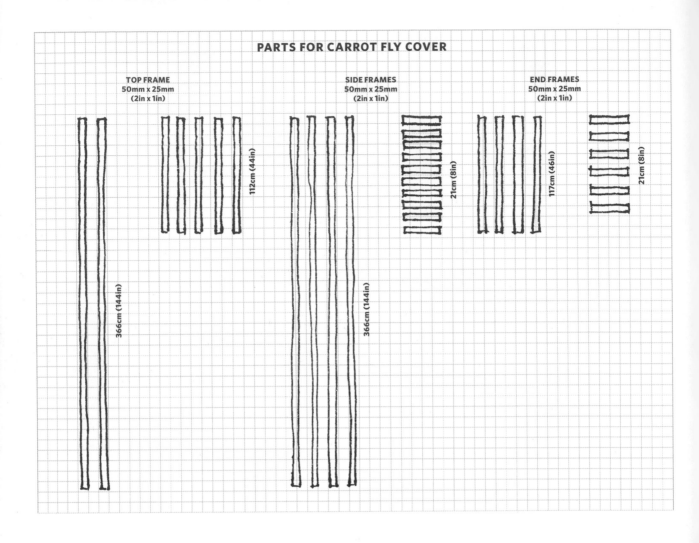

PARTS FOR CARROT FLY COVER

TOP FRAME
50mm x 25mm
(2in x 1in)

112cm (44in)

366cm (144in)

SIDE FRAMES
50mm x 25mm
(2in x 1in)

21cm (8in)

366cm (144in)

END FRAMES
50mm x 25mm
(2in x 1in)

117cm (46in)

21cm (8in)

Making the carrot fly cover

STEP 1 SMOOTH AND CUT THE TIMBER

Use a plane or sanding sheet to smooth
the rough edges of all the timbers so that
the netting doesn't snag. It is easier to do
this while the timber is in long lengths.
Mark the timber, with the square and
pencil, and cut to the sizes required.
Remember to sand any cut ends too.

STEP 2 MAKE A MARKING CARD

Mark a 50mm x 25mm (2in x 1in) piece of
card with two points at 10mm (³/₈in) from
each end. Use this to mark drilling points
in each end of all the 21cm (8in) pieces
of timber and in each end of all the 112cm
(44in) pieces of timber.

STEP 3 DRILL PILOT HOLES IN MARKED ENDS

Using the 4mm (⁵/₃₂in) bit, make holes
10mm (³/₈in) deep in the end of the
timbers you marked in Step 2. These pilot
holes will guide the screws into the correct
position. Note: it is always safest to hold
timber in a workbench clamp or vice when
drilling to avoid accidents.

STEP 4 MARK CLEARANCE HOLES

Use the marking card to mark the two ends of all 366cm (144in) lengths, and all 117cm (46in) lengths (as shown). Mark two drilling points at 92cm (36in), 183cm (72in) and 274cm (108in) along one edge of all 366cm (144in) pieces and at the midpoint of the 117cm (46in) pieces.

STEP 5 DRILL CLEARANCE HOLES

Use a 5mm ($^3/_{16}$ in) bit to drill clearance holes through the points marked in Step 4. Choose the two pieces of 366cm (144in) timber with the straightest and flattest edges to fit against the raised bed. Use any bowed lengths for the top sections, where a flat fit isn't essential.

STEP 6 ASSEMBLE FIVE FRAMES

Assemble all five frames using 5mm x 100mm (No 10 x 4in) screws at the pre-drilled points. The finished top frame is 366cm x 122cm (144in x 48in), the two finished side frames are 366cm x 31cm (144in x 12in) and two finished end frames are 117cm x 31cm (46in x 12in).

STEP 7 COVER FRAMES WITH NETTING

Spread out the netting and lay the frames on top. Cut netting to fit each frame, allowing an extra 10mm ($^3/_8$ in) all round. Spread the netting over the inside surface of each frame, fold the extra 10mm ($^3/_8$ in) over to give edges a double layer, and fix with plenty of staples.

STEP 8 FIX ROPE TO ONE SIDE

Stretch the netting so it is wrinkle-free when stapled, but don't stretch it so tight that it pulls against the staples and tears. Fit the three pieces of rope at equal spaces along one of the side frames. Hammer in the small fencing staples to hold the rope in place (as shown).

STEP 9 ASSEMBLE THE COVER

Use two 5mm x 60mm (No 10 x 2$^3/_8$in) screws at the end of each side to assemble the lower frame. The sides overlap the end pieces, but take care to avoid colliding with other screws. Fix the top onto the lower frame with 4mm x 40mm (No 8 x 1$^1/_2$in) screws, set 60cm (24in) apart.

STEP 10 FIT A GASKET

If the cover is to go over a raised bed, then it is a good idea to fit a 'gasket' to fill any gaps between the two. Any flexible, durable material, such as underlay, folded netting, or rubber inner tube, will work. Staple strips of suitable material around the bottom edge of the frame.

STEP 11 FIT THE HINGES

Put the cover in place over the raised bed. Corner posts on the bed can help to keep the cover aligned. Hinges go on the opposite side to the one where you fitted the lengths of rope. Fix one hinge in the middle and one 30cm (12in) from each end of the cover and frame.

STEP 12 ATTACH CLEATS

Fix three cleats to the side of the raised bed. These should line up with the ropes, which wind round the cleats neatly to close the cover. The cover should fit perfectly in place, leaving no gaps for the flies to get through. To open, unwind the rope and tip the cover back on the hinges.

SOWING AND GROWING TIPS FOR THE CARROT FLY COVER

Grow carrots under this cover or use it to protect parsnips, early onions, and cabbage crops from a range of flying pests and frost.

After harvesting your carrots you can replant the bed with autumn onions.

- **You can also make** the cover to sit directly on the soil, but you should leave an extra 30cm (12in) of netting to lap onto the ground all around. Weigh down this extra material with bricks or stones to keep the frame in place and the carrot flies out.
- **Sow maincrop carrots** in mid-spring in drills 15mm (1/2in) deep and allow 30cm (12in) between rows. Sow seed at around one good pinch per 60cm (24in). Thin seedlings later if lots grow.
- **Put a little fine leafmould**, or compost, in the bottom of drills before sowing and keep the bed watered in dry weather.
- **Protect against slugs** and snails from 12 days after sowing until plants are around 12cm (5in) tall.
- **Thin out plants** when leaves are around 15cm (6in) tall. Allow the strongest ones to grow on at a distance of 10cm (4in) apart. Firm any soil that is disturbed around remaining plants. Choose a dull day for this job and open the cover for as short a time as possible. Use any thinned roots that are large enough to eat – the foliage can also be eaten as a microgreen, or bury removed leaves in the compost heap so they don't attract carrot flies to the garden.
- **Start harvesting** the roots from midsummer onwards. Raise the cover as little as possible when lifting the roots.
- **Try replanting** with autumn onion sets or garlic when the carrots are lifted. These can do very well with some winter protection and you can move the cover to a new bed for carrots when spring comes around.

Make the frame to fit the space in your garden.

Enjoy a perfect crop of carrots free from fly damage.

You will need

**For a frame measuring
170cm x 155cm x 70cm (67in x 61in x 28in)**

- **Timber**
  - 2 x top uprights: 40cm x 50mm x 25mm
  (16in x 2in x 1in)
  - 1 x top horizontal: 155cm x 50mm x 25mm
  (61in x 2in x 1in)
  - 4 x front uprights: 150cm x 50mm x 25mm
  (59in x 2in x 1in)
  - 2 x front horizontals: 150cm x 50mm x 25mm
  (59in x 2in x 1in)
  - 2 x doorposts: 164cm (64in) approx. x 50mm x 25mm
  (2in x 1in) cut to correct length when the frame is in place
- **Polythene**
  - 320cm x 275cm (126in x 108in) approx.
  Heavy-duty, clear
- **Fixings**
  - 12 x 4mm x 40mm (No 8 x 1½in) screws
  - 14 x 5mm x 80mm (No 10 x 3¼in) screws
  - 2 x hooks
  - 2 x rings
  - 2 x wall fixings
  - Large washers

TOOLS

- Tape measure
- Saw
- Drill, with 5mm (³/₁₆in), 4mm (⁵/₃₂in) and 3mm (¹/₈in) drill bits, plus masonry bit
- Screwdriver
- Staple gun and staples
- Stanley knife
- Square
- Pencil
- Sanding sheet and block
- Card

This robust structure works as a little greenhouse. Tender plants benefit from the extra heat retained in the wall behind and the frame can be removed if they outgrow it.

A lean-to polyframe makes good use of a sunny wall. The wall warms up through the day and releases heat at night into the enclosed polythene-clad space, creating a more constant heat for tender plants, such as peppers, tomatoes and aubergines (eggplants). We have had great success growing all of these crops in our lean-to polyframe. You can also use the space to raise early spring plants for growing on outdoors or add shelves if you want to start lots of seeds in pots and trays.

The frame is easy to make and will last for many years if you use heavy-duty polythene. You will also need a masonry drill bit and some sturdy fixings to hold the frame to the wall so it doesn't blow away in a strong wind.

If you want to make a longer structure, simply increase the length of all the horizontal timbers.

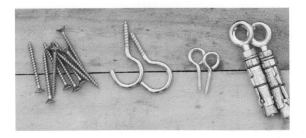

Some useful fixings for this project, left to right: 4mm x 40mm (No 8 x 1½in) screws, hooks, rings, and wall fixings.

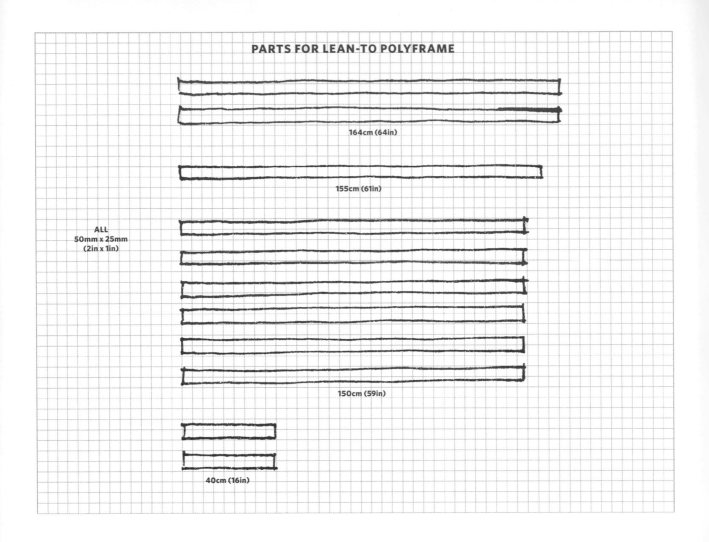

PARTS FOR LEAN-TO POLYFRAME

164cm (64in)

155cm (61in)

ALL
50mm x 25mm
(2in x 1in)

150cm (59in)

40cm (16in)

Making the lean-to polyframe

STEP 1 SOME PREPARATION

Use the block and sanding sheet to smooth all rough edges on the timbers. It is important that splinters won't tear the polythene. Make a marking card 25mm x 50mm (1in x 2in) marked with two points 10mm ($^3/_8$in) in from each end and make holes large enough for a pencil point.

STEP 2 MARK DRILLING POINTS

With the aid of the marking card and pencil, mark the following drilling points: into the grain at each end of one 155cm (61in) and two 150cm (59in) lengths of timber; at each end of the broad face of two 150cm (59in) timbers and at one end of two 40cm (16in) lengths of timber.

STEP 3 DRILL CLEARANCE AND PILOT HOLES

Use the 4mm ($^5/_{32}$in) bit to make pilot holes at all points marked in the 155cm (61in) and 150cm (59in) timbers. Use the 5mm ($^3/_{16}$in) drill bit to make clearance holes at all points in the other timbers. Join four 150cm (59in) pieces together with 5mm x 80mm (No 10 x 3$^1/_4$in) screws to make the front frame.

STEP 4 FIX POLYTHENE TO THE FRONT FRAME

With the Stanley knife, cut the heavy duty polythene sheet to size. Leave surplus polythene at the edges to lap onto the ground and two loose pieces at each side of the frame to make side door flaps. Stretch the polythene across the front frame and staple in place.

STEP 5 SANDWICH POLYTHENE ALONG THE SIDES

Fix a 150cm (59in) length of timber onto each side of the frame using five 4mm x 40mm (No 8 x 1½in) screws. With the 3mm (⅛in) drill bit, make pilot holes if needed. In this way, the polythene is sandwiched between the two timbers so the staples won't pull out.

STEP 6 ASSEMBLE THE TOP FRAME

Assemble the top frame using 5mm x 80mm (No 10 x 3¼in) screws to fix through the 40cm (16in) pieces and into the ends of the 155cm (61in) piece to make a three-sided unit. Cover with polythene; staple in place, allowing excess to hang down on the empty side of the frame.

STEP 7 JOIN THE TWO FRAMES

Drill and fix one 5mm x 80mm (No 10 x 3¼in) screw at each side, to join the top frame to the front frame. Set the desired angle between the two sections, then staple and trim excess polythene where the top frame joins to the front frame.

STEP 8 SECURE WALL FIXINGS

Put the frame in place and mark where fixings will go. Use a suitable masonry bit, or timber drill bit, depending on the structure of the wall. Knock fixings in and tighten them until they are secure. Fix a washer and screw through the eye of the wall fixing into the top frame.

STEP 9 MAKE DOOR CATCHES

Screw hooks into the top ends of the upright door posts and put rings at a corresponding point in the sides of the top frame. You close the door by hooking these two together and open it by unhooking them. Make cuts into the corners so the polythene 'skirt' lies flat on the ground.

STEP 10 FINISH THE DOORS

Cut the door posts to the right length so they fit between the hook and the ground. Wrap the edge of a polythene door flap around a door post and staple in place. Repeat for the second door. Weigh down the plastic 'skirt' on the ground with stones, bricks or other heavy items.

TIPS FOR USING AND GROWING CROPS IN THE LEAN-TO POLYFRAME

Roll the doors back and prop them open against the front frame on sunny or warm days to provide ventilation and ensure plants don't overheat.

Peppers grow well in a lean-to frame, and are easy to access through the side 'doors'.

- **The gaps at the top** of the door flaps allow a small amount of ventilation. This is an important feature in an enclosed space that is exposed to the sun.
- **A watering can** with a long spout is ideal for delivering water to pots behind the frame. The door space is wide enough to reach in comfortably and access all plants.
- **Peppers, aubergines (eggplants) and tomatoes** do well if grown in large pots or growing bags in the polyframe. These heat-loving plants will produce plenty of fruits if they are kept fed and watered and not overcrowded. Buy small plants and don't put them into the frame until late spring, or early summer if the spring weather is particularly cold.
- **Start an early courgette** (zucchini) plant in a 30cm (12in) pot. It can produce early fruits in late spring if sheltered behind the frame. Move the pot outside as soon as weather conditions permit.
- **Keep an eye** on things and remove the frame, or move plants outside, if they outgrow the space.
- **Try sowing rocket**, mizuna and mustard greens in pots behind the frame. Sow in early autumn for some of the most reliable winter leaves.
- **Plants grow fast** here so remember to provide a liquid feed every couple of weeks when growth is rapid or fruits are swelling.

Water pots of plants regularly, as the hot atmosphere will dry them out quickly.

Double compost bin

A compost bin is a vital part of any vegetable garden. Some try to disguise their bins but this beautiful handmade double unit is good enough to put on display. Easy to use, it also produces great compost, and the solid construction will last for years.

It is worth pausing for a moment before making a new compost bin. This is an important structure in the garden and you shouldn't rush the planning stage. Think about the best place to put it: a short distance from kitchen door and garden beds to make trips to and fro easier, avoiding slopes if possible, and where your bin will not upset the neighbours.

If you are treating yourself to these lovely compost bins, be sure to buy strong and durable materials. The site also needs to be prepared well and choose an area that can be accessed easily. You may also want to set aside a weekend to complete the project, spreading the work over both days so the concrete has time to set.

There is a degree of precision in the construction and you should make the bin level and straight. No stage is difficult, but it is worth being patient and getting each step right for a strong, functional and aesthetically pleasing result. We have also included the recipe for perfect compost at the end of the project to make all your hard work worthwhile.

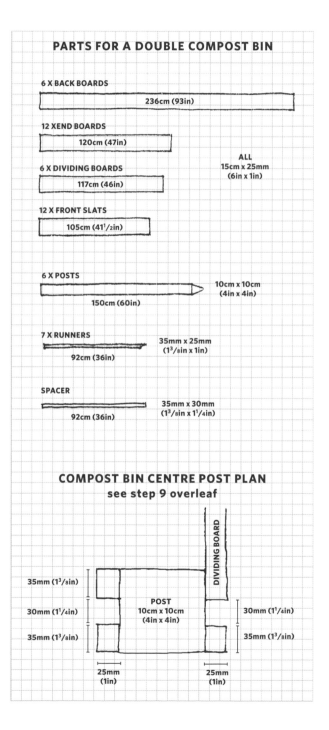

PARTS FOR A DOUBLE COMPOST BIN

6 X BACK BOARDS
236cm (93in)

12 X END BOARDS
120cm (47in)

6 X DIVIDING BOARDS
117cm (46in)

ALL
15cm x 25mm
(6in x 1in)

12 X FRONT SLATS
105cm (41$\frac{1}{2}$in)

6 X POSTS
150cm (60in)

10cm x 10cm
(4in x 4in)

7 X RUNNERS
92cm (36in)

35mm x 25mm
(1$\frac{3}{8}$in x 1in)

SPACER
92cm (36in)

35mm x 30mm
(1$\frac{3}{8}$in x 1$\frac{1}{4}$in)

COMPOST BIN CENTRE POST PLAN
see step 9 overleaf

DIVIDING BOARD

35mm (1$\frac{3}{8}$in)

30mm (1$\frac{1}{4}$in)

35mm (1$\frac{3}{8}$in)

POST
10cm x 10cm
(4in x 4in)

30mm (1$\frac{1}{4}$in)

35mm (1$\frac{3}{8}$in)

25mm
(1in)

25mm
(1in)

You will need

**For a double bin measuring
245cm x 127cm x 100cm (96in x 50in x 40in)**

- **Timber**
This bin is made from untreated European larch boards and spruce posts treated with Tanalith E
  - 6 x back boards: 236cm x 15cm x 25mm (93in x 6in x 1in)
  - 12 x end boards: 120cm x 15cm x 25mm (47in x 6in x 1in)
  - 6 x dividing boards: 117cm x 15cm x 25mm (46in x 6in x 1in)
  - 12 x front slats, cut these to fit at Step 11: 105cm x 15cm x 25mm (41$\frac{1}{2}$in x 6in x 1in)
  - 6 x posts: 150cm x 10cm x 10cm (60in x 4in x 4in)
  - 7 x runners, with one end cut to a neat wedge: 92cm x 35mm x 25mm (36in x 1$\frac{3}{8}$in x 1in)
  - 1 x spacer: 92cm x 35mm x 30mm (36in x 1$\frac{3}{8}$in x 1$\frac{1}{4}$in)
  - Long lengths of spare timber suitable for bracing
- **Nails**
65mm (2$\frac{1}{2}$in) galvanised ovals
- **Screws**
4mm x 40mm (No 8 x 1$\frac{1}{2}$in) stainless steel
- **Fill material**
  - Small stones, hardcore, or concrete, for post holes
  - Concrete blocks, or flat paving slabs, for base

TOOLS

- Long straight crowbar
- Tape measure
- String
- Marking sticks
- Digging tools (a post hole borer is useful if you have one)
- Sledgehammer
- Drill with 3mm (1/8in) bit and screwdriver bit
- Hammer
- Pencil
- Square
- Spirit level
- Saw

Making the double compost bin

Level the site. Mark the positions of the centres of the posts with sticks and string. The front and back corner sticks are 230cm (90½in) apart; the ends 114cm (45in) apart. Mark the middle posts with sticks 115cm (45½in) from the corners.

STEP 2   DIG HOLES FOR POSTS

Check that diagonals are equal then dig holes to a depth of 50cm (20in). You should not have any difficulty on light soil, but on stony soil you may have to use a crowbar to lever out rocks. The narrower the holes, the less filling material is needed.

STEP 3   DRILL HOLES IN BACK BOARDS

Use the 3mm (⅛in) drill bit to make two holes at each end of the 236cm (93in) boards. Make the holes 25mm (1in) from the ends and sides. Drilling prevents boards splitting when nailed. Drill two boards at a time if your bit is long enough.

STEP 4   ASSEMBLE THE BACK PANEL

Lay three posts on the ground at the required spacing for the back three holes. Lay a board in position, 5cm (2in) from the top of each post, and nail in place. Check that the panel is square. Nail on five more boards, with minimal gaps in between.

STEP 5   INSTALL THE BACK PANEL

Lift the back panel into position and place posts in the holes. Keep it vertical and level: use a spare timber to hold the panel and secure this to a nearby structure, temporary post, or tree. Leave a gap between the bottom board and the ground.

STEP 6   FILL AROUND THE POSTS

Raise any post that's too deep in a hole by pushing a stone under it. When straight, fill the corner holes with hardcore. Use a sledgehammer to ram down large stones and pack smaller stones around them (use protective eyewear and don't hit too hard).

STEP 7   POSITION THE FRONT POSTS

Put the front posts into the holes. Use the spirit level to ensure they're vertical and level. Measure diagonals and move posts around if necessary to centre them in the holes. Use spare lengths of timber to hold everything in place temporarily.

STEP 8   FIX END BOARDS AND POSTS

Drill and nail six 120cm (47in) boards onto each of the ends of the bins. Make sure these are level and square. Pour concrete around the base of the centre front post and leave to set for 24–48 hours. If this post moves, the slats will not slide in freely.

STEP 9   ATTACH DIVIDING BOARDS AND FIT BASE

Drill and use screws to secure the front edges of the dividing boards to the central post. The board edges should line up vertically – see plan on p.173 – against which slats will slide. Drill and nail the back edges. Lay blocks or paving in the base.

STEP 10 FIX THE RUNNERS

Fix two vertical runners to each front corner post. Use four evenly spaced screws per runner and the spacer to create the gap between the runners (as shown). Fix one runner to the centre post; the edge of the dividing boards acts as a second runner.

STEP 11 START TO FILL AND FIT THE FRONT SLATS

Cut the front slats about 15mm (¹/₂in) less than the width between posts, so they slide freely between the runners. If the posts splay you may need to cut each slat to a different length. Fill the compost bin in layers; slide in the slats as the heap builds.

LAYING DOWN THE LAW FOR PERFECT COMPOST

Layers. Fill the bin in layers to get a mix of nitrogen-rich and carbon-rich materials: ensure layers are no more than 15cm (6in) deep and make the nitrogen-rich ones thinner than carbon ones.

Aerate. Keep air in the mix: when one side fills, turn the contents into the other empty side, or use an aeration tool.

Water. Ensure the mix is damp: a dry compost heap will not rot but a waterlogged one will stagnate and smell.

TIPS FOR MAKING GREAT COMPOST IN THE BIN

This two-bin system means that one side is always being filled with new materials, while the other side is covered and decomposing, or emptied out as finished compost is used.

Add some worm-rich compost from the side that's rotting down to the side that you are filling with fresh material.

- **Alternate carbon and nitrogen** layers in the bin. The ideal ratio for these is 30:1 for large heaps and 15:1 for small heaps.
- **Carbon-rich materials** include straw, cardboard, leaves, paper, wood shavings, hay and dried plant material.
- **Nitrogen-rich materials** include grass clippings, manure, seaweed, most kitchen waste, tea leaves and urine.
- **Put a layer of plants** with strong stems in the base and don't pack layers down: plenty of air in the heap helps it to heat up.
- **Worms and compost** are perfect partners: add a scoop of lovely worm-rich compost from decomposed material to the fresh stuff.
- **A thin layer of lime** will help balance the acidity (pH) of the compost.
- **When one side is full**, turn the contents over into the empty side and cap the pile off with a layer of manure. You can put finished compost into bags at one side if you need to turn the pile before the second side is empty.
- **Cover the bin** when it is full and leave the contents to break down. Compost will break down faster in the summer than it does in the winter and thin materials break down more quickly than thick chunky ones. You can get coarse compost from an active heap within a few weeks, but the longer you leave it, the better it gets.
- **Don't put any meat**, fish, or cooked food into the heap, as these will attract rats and other vermin.

Garden caddy

You don't have to be a carpenter to create this beautiful, useful garden caddy. Nor do you have to be a master gardener to enjoy loading it up with tools and plants, or to use it to harvest your delicious garden vegetables.

Make one lovely caddy for yourself and another as a gift for a gardening friend. It provides plenty of space for tools and plants, and stands level and steady on the ground. It certainly beats stuffing tools in pockets, or harvesting into the scooped-up front of a sweater, and it's perfect for carrying your equipment around the garden with ease.

This practical project needs only a few tools and some scraps of wood. You can vary the dimensions if you want to make the caddy larger or smaller, but keep the weight of the finished item in mind before deciding to scale things up too much.

We made this particular caddy from pine, which is easy to work and you can treat it with paint, a colourful wood stain, varnish or oils for a professional finish.

The caddy is ideal for collecting harvested crops.

You will need

**For a caddy measuring
52cm x 28cm (20¹/₂in x 11in)**

- **Timber**
  - 2 x long sides: 52.5cm x 14cm x 16mm (20³/₄in x 5¹/₂in x ⁵/₈in)
  - 2 x short sides: 28.5cm x 14cm x 16mm (11¹/₄in x 5¹/₂in x ⁵/₈in)
  - 2 x inserts: 24cm x 12.4cm x 10mm (9¹/₂in x 5in x ³/₈in)
  - 1 x insert: 18cm x 12.4cm x 10mm (7in x 5in x ³/₈in)
  - 2 x handle uprights: 40cm x 32mm x 16mm (16in x 1¹/₄in x ⁵/₈in)
  - 1 x broom handle 57cm x 25mm diameter (22¹/₂in x 1in)
- **Plywood**
  - 51.5cm x 28cm x 6mm (20¹/₄in x 11in x ¹/₄in) base
- **Screws**
  - 2 x 5mm x 60mm (No 10 x 2³/₈in)
  - 4 x 5mm x 30mm (No 10 x 1¹/₄in)
- **Nails**
  - 50mm (2in) galvanised ovals
  - 30mm (1¹/₄in) galvanised panel pins

TOOLS

- Drill with 5.5mm (⁷/₃₂in), 3mm (¹/₈in) and 1.5mm (¹/₁₆in) drill bits
- Countersink tool or bit
- Hammer
- Jigsaw
- Nail punch
- Pencil
- Square
- Tape measure
- Sanding sheet

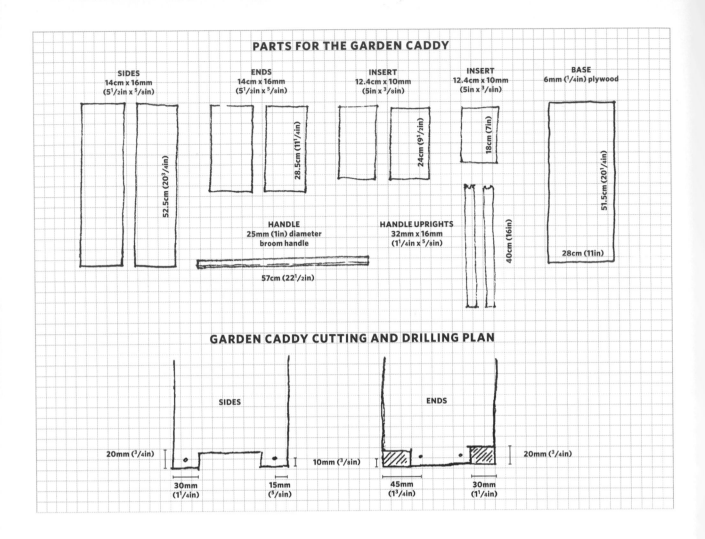

PARTS FOR THE GARDEN CADDY

SIDES
14cm x 16mm
(5¹/₂in x ⁵/₈in)
52.5cm (20³/₄in)

ENDS
14cm x 16mm
(5¹/₂in x ⁵/₈in)
28.5cm (11¹/₄in)

INSERT
12.4cm x 10mm
(5in x ³/₈in)
24cm (9¹/₂in)

INSERT
12.4cm x 10mm
(5in x ³/₈in)
18cm (7in)

BASE
6mm (¹/₄in) plywood
51.5cm (20¹/₄in)
28cm (11in)

HANDLE
25mm (1in) diameter
broom handle
57cm (22¹/₂in)

HANDLE UPRIGHTS
32mm x 16mm
(1¹/₄in x ⁵/₈in)
40cm (16in)

GARDEN CADDY CUTTING AND DRILLING PLAN

SIDES
20mm (³/₄in)
30mm (1¹/₄in)
15mm (⁵/₈in)

ENDS
10mm (³/₈in)
20mm (³/₄in)
45mm (1³/₄in)
30mm (1¹/₄in)

Making the garden caddy

STEP 1 CHOOSE THE TIMBER

Decide which edge of the sides and ends will touch the base piece and mark triangles on these with a pencil. The triangles act as a reference point so you always know that pieces are the right way up when working on them. Choose flat, unflawed timber for the ends and sides.

STEP 2 MARK CUT LINES AND DRILLING POINTS

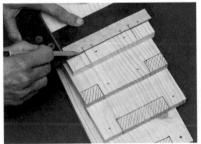

Stick masking tape on the edge of the square; mark points as shown above. Transfer onto timber: mark lines 30mm (1¹/₄in) from each side and 20mm (³/₄in) from ends; drilling points 10mm (³/₈in) from end, and 15mm (⁵/₈in) from each edge of the sides, or 45mm (1³/₄in) of the ends.

STEP 3 CUT ALONG MARKED LINES

Use a clamp to hold the timber steady. Cut along the lines to leave a tongue sticking out at each end of the short sides and a corresponding cutout in the long sides. When using a jigsaw, first cut a curve round the internal corners, then go back to cut out the right angles.

STEP 4 DRILL CLEARANCE AND PILOT HOLES

With the 3mm (1/8in) bit, drill clearance holes at the marked points. Put sides together so tongues slot into cutouts at right angles. Tap a nail through clearance holes to mark the wood grain of the ends beneath. Take sides apart; make pilot holes at these points with a 1.5mm (1/16in) bit.

STEP 5 ASSEMBLE THE SIDES

Sand any rough edges. Slot tongues into cutouts so the sides push together and all joints are tight. Hammer 50mm (2in) oval nails through the clearance holes and into the pre-drilled pilot holes. Use a punch to knock the top of the nails just below the surface of the timber.

STEP 6 FIT THE BASE

Use the 1.5mm (1/16in) drill bit to make sixteen evenly spaced guide holes 8mm (5/16in) from the edge, all the way round the plywood. Check that the triangles drawn in Step 1 are against the base. Use panel pins to fit the base. Punch pinheads down just below the surface.

STEP 7 CUT OUT SLOTS

Cut slots in the 18cm (7in) insert and one 24cm (9½in) insert. Mark the midpoint on the long edge of each insert. Measure 5mm (3/16in) out from each side of the midpoint and draw parallel lines to half the width of the board. This forms a 10mm x 62mm (3/8in x 2½in) slot.

STEP 8 FIT THE INSERTS

Link the slotted inserts together to form a cross. Place this at one end of the caddy. Drill and use panel pins to fit the remaining 24cm (9½in) insert piece across the end to form four equal compartments. Optional: drill and fix pins through the base to hold this section in place.

STEP 9 MARK AND CUT THE ENDS OF THE HANDLE

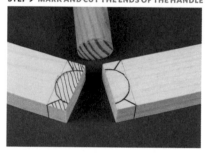

Draw a semi-circle at the end of each upright using the end of the broom handle as a template. Draw lines for the cut out areas as shown and crosshatch areas to be removed. Use a clamp to hold the upright firmly and 'nibble' at the inner rim of the lines with a jigsaw blade for a neat curve.

STEP 10 DRILL AND COUNTERSINK HOLES

Mark drilling points 18mm (3/4in) from each end of the broom handle. To prevent the drill skidding, start with the 1.5mm (1/16in) drill bit to make a small pilot hole, then follow with the 5.5mm (7/32in) bit. Use the countersink tool to make a neat indentation for the screw heads.

STEP 11 FIX THE HANDLE SIDES

Make holes for screws, 25mm (1in) and 11cm (4¼in) from bottom ends of handle upright with a 5.5mm (7/32in) bit and countersink. Set these centrally on each short side of the caddy. Hold in place with a 30mm (1¼in) screw, and ensure they're vertical before fixing the second screw.

STEP 12 FIT THE HANDLE

Use the 3mm (1/8in) drill bit to make pilot holes in the end grain of the uprights. Then, with the 60mm (2³/8in) screws, fix the handle in place. Make sure all joints are tight and that the handle is rigid. The caddy should sit level on the ground. Paint or stain the caddy as required.

TIPS FOR USING THE GARDEN CADDY

Paint or varnish the caddy to help the wood last longer, or leave it untreated and store it undercover when not in use.

The caddy is ideal for carrying tools and equipment around the garden.

- **Use the caddy** to organise your gardening activities. Simply load up the compartments with the things that you need and you will have everything close to hand when it comes to those fiddly garden tasks. If you spot a stray raspberry cane, you can soon tie it back, or if there is a cauliflower ready to harvest, you won't need to run to the house for a knife to cut through the stem.
- **Some of our favourite things** to keep in the caddy include string and other ties, secateurs, a hand fork and trowel, a cutting and harvesting tool such as a garden knife, and garden gloves. In spring, when beds are planted, it may also hold a pH metre to make sure each crop is planted in the soil it will most enjoy.
- **Load up** the caddy with pots or bulbs at planting time, and the means to plant them so you have a complete kit. It's useful for garlic and onion sets and for trays of brassicas, or container plants. You can even fill one of the sections with packets of seeds, filed in planting order, and keep some labels and a pen in another compartment to ensure all rows are clearly labelled after sowing.
- **Use the main compartment** of the caddy as a trug for harvesting: fill it with apples or beans, or harvested fresh salad leaves.
- **Make a few** caddies as presents for gardening friends and relatives, or simply use them to store a range of different items in the shed, ready to pick up and go when you need them.

Use the large compartment to gather fresh crops that are easily damaged or bruised, such as lettuce leaves and tomatoes (right).

Growing bag cradle

This stylish cradle will transform a growing bag into a beautiful and practical feature. You can use the finished article as a herb bed, a strawberry tray, or for growing peas and beans up canes fitted into it.

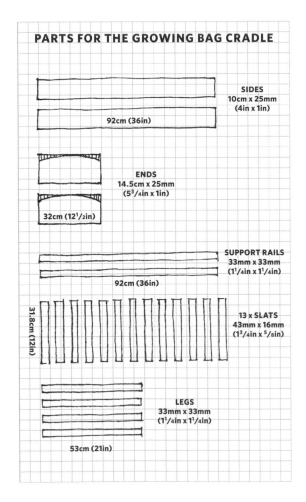

PARTS FOR THE GROWING BAG CRADLE

SIDES
10cm x 25mm
(4in x 1in)

92cm (36in)

ENDS
14.5cm x 25mm
(5³/₄in x 1in)

32cm (12¹/₂in)

SUPPORT RAILS
33mm x 33mm
(1¹/₄in x 1¹/₄in)

92cm (36in)

31.8cm (12in)

13 x SLATS
43mm x 16mm
(1³/₄in x ⁵/₈in)

LEGS
33mm x 33mm
(1¹/₄in x 1¹/₄in)

53cm (21in)

Growing bags are really useful aids in the edible garden and they can create an instant veg patch in any back yard. These compost-filled growing modules are most often used for tomatoes, but they can be used to grow almost any crop that takes your fancy.

You will need to keep your growing bags watered well and add fertiliser when the original supply runs short, but these tasks don't take long and the rewards are great. The main problem with growing bags is that they aren't very attractive and they are also difficult to move without disturbing the plants. In addition, there's the question of how to support tall crops if the growing bag is on paving stones or concrete. The answer, of course, is to make this cradle. A beautiful container with many uses, it's a good height to work with, includes brackets for canes, and it's easy to move.

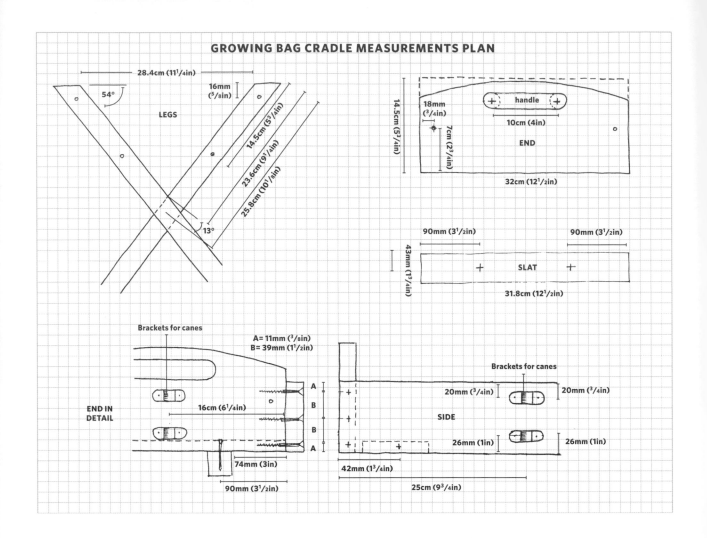

GROWING BAG CRADLE MEASUREMENTS PLAN

LEGS
54°
28.4cm (11¹/₄in)
16mm (⁵/₈in)
14.5cm (5³/₄in)
23.6cm (9¹/₄in)
25.8cm (10¹/₈in)
13°

END
18mm (³/₄in)
handle
14.5cm (5³/₄in)
7cm (2³/₄in)
10cm (4in)
32cm (12¹/₂in)

SLAT
90mm (3¹/₂in)
90mm (3¹/₂in)
43mm (1³/₄in)
31.8cm (12¹/₂in)

Brackets for canes
A= 11mm (³/₈in)
B= 39mm (1¹/₂in)
END IN DETAIL
16cm (6¹/₄in)
A
B
B
A
74mm (3in)
90mm (3¹/₂in)

Brackets for canes
SIDE
20mm (³/₄in)
20mm (³/₄in)
26mm (1in)
26mm (1in)
42mm (1³/₄in)
25cm (9³/₄in)

Making the growing bag cradle

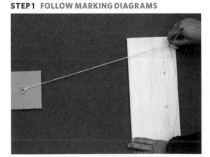

Measure and mark all drilling points as shown on the measurements plan above. Also mark a curve on the top edge of the two end pieces. A length of string secured at one end, and a pencil tied at the other, will help you to draw an even curve (or choose another shape).

Use the jigsaw to cut the curved tops. With the 25mm (1in) bit, first drill holes at the points marked on the end sections for the handle. Use the jigsaw to cut between the drilled holes to make the handle slots. Sand all the rough edges until smooth to the touch.

Make clearance holes at the points marked on the side pieces of the growing bag cradle using the 5mm (³/₁₆in) drill bit. Use a countersink bit in each hole to make a shallow depression so the heads of the screws will sink just below the surface of the timber.

STEP 4 FIT BRACKETS (OPTIONAL)

Use the 2mm (5/64in) drill bit to make pilot holes for brackets at points marked on the inside of the sides and ends (see diagram opposite). Squeeze the brackets if necessary so they fit neatly round canes. Use 3.5mm x 16mm (No 6 x 5/8in) screws to fix the brackets in place.

STEP 5 ASSEMBLE THE FRAME

Assemble the four sides of the frame using 5mm x 60mm screws (No 10 x 2³/8in). Use a 3mm (1/8in) drill to make pilot holes if not using self-drilling screws. Note: three screws are used at each corner so the frame doesn't pull apart if the legs are dragged or knocked.

STEP 6 FIX THE BOTTOM RAILS

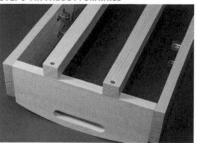

Use the 5mm (³/16in) bit to drill clearance holes at the ends of the rails. Tap a nail through the holes to mark drilling points and drill pilot holes at these points (unless using self-drilling screws). Fix 5mm x 60mm (No 10 x 2³/8in) screws through clearance holes into the end pieces.

STEP 7 FIT THE SLATS

With the 3mm (1/8in) bit, drill clearance holes in the slats as marked. Knock nails into each of these holes before positioning in the base of the frame. Allow 27mm (1¹/16in) gaps between slats; nail in place. Screw through the side pieces and into the two end and middle slats for extra rigidity.

STEP 8 MARK ANGLES ON LEGS

Use the bevel square to mark a 52 degree angle on each end of the legs. Saw across the marked lines. This angle means that the tops and feet are level when the legs are joined in a cross. The finished cradle will then stand steady, without rocking, when placed on a level surface.

STEP 9 MARK HALVING JOINTS

First use the angle bevel to mark cutting lines as in the measurement details diagram opposite. Measure and mark a stop line at half the depth of the timber and shade in the area to cut out. Use the handsaw to make several cuts down through the shaded area to the stop line.

STEP 10 CHISEL OUT THE JOINTS

Always hold timber in a clamp and take great care when using sharp tools. Use the mallet and chisel to clear surplus timber from the joints. The more saw cuts you have made, the easier this is. Aim for smooth level surfaces in order to produce neat joints in the finished leg pieces.

STEP 11 ASSEMBLE THE LEGS

Use a 4mm (5/32in) bit to make clearance holes and a 3mm (1/8in) bit to make pilot holes (if needed) as shown on the diagram. Use 4mm x 50mm (No 8 x 2in) screws to assemble the legs as shown. Note: you can also use glue in this joint if you want additional strength.

STEP 12 FIT THE LEGS

Fix the legs to the ends of the frame with 4mm x 50mm (No 8 x 2in) screws. Drill and screw from the inside of the frame. For extra strength use 5mm x 80mm (No 10 x 3 ¹/4in) screws to fix the legs onto the ends of the rails. The cradle is now ready to paint or stain.

TIPS FOR USING THE GROWING BAG CRADLE

Paint or stain the finished cradle before putting the growing bag in place and planting it with your favourite vegetables and fruit. Then set it on a level surface.

Try growing runner beans in pots instead of a growing bag in the cradle.

- **Cover the growing bag** with material to disguise the ugly plastic; we used a piece of black weed-control fabric. Tuck the material right underneath so the bag weighs it down and cut through both layers when making planting holes.
- **Paint the wood** to match your garden theme or style. Choose a product that is designed for outdoor use and one that allows the grain of the wood to show through.
- **Plant the growing bag** with herbs and keep the cradle near the kitchen door. We put rosemary, sage, thyme, and a curry plant in this one. Pick leaves regularly to keep the plants compact so they don't outgrow the space too quickly.
- **Bamboo canes** slot into the brackets inside the cradle and tie at the top. Grow climbing beans to twine up them or use them as a support for cordon tomato plants. Individual beans grow well in 20cm (8in) pots, if you want to fill the cradle with these rather than a growing bag.
- **Strawberries**, aubergines (eggplants) and melons all grow well in individual pots, which you can push through holes cut in the growing bag. This provides extra compost and feeding capacity as plants grow.
- **Growing bag nutrients** are usually depleted after six to eight weeks if plants are putting on good growth. For greedy plants, use a liquid feed every seven to ten days after this.
- **You can make** just the top part of the cradle and rest this on the ground, or on bricks, if you prefer not to make the legs.

RIGHT You can grow a range of herbs by the kitchen door in the growing bag. For a neater finish, cover it so plastic is hidden.

OPPOSITE Bamboo canes for beans slot into the brackets.

Glossary

Abrasive sheet
Paper or cloth coated with abrasive grit. Also known as sandpaper.

Alkathene
Commonly used type of semi-rigid polyethylene water pipe.

Batten
A strip of wood, roughly 50mm x 25mm (2in x 1in) in cross-section, used in these projects. Frequently used in the construction industry to support slates and tiles.

Bevel
A slanting edge.

Bradawl
A tool with a sharp point that can be pushed into timber to make a guide hole for drilling, or for guiding a nail or screw. It is sometimes called a gimlet or spike.

Chamfer
A shallow-angled cut across the corner between two edges.

Cleat
A metal fixing to which rope can be secured.

Cloche
A structure for covering and protecting young plants. Usually domed and made of clear polythene, plastic or glass.

Cold frame
A semi-permanent low-level structure, usually with a glass lid, that provides a protected growing space for plants.

Counterbore
A deep broad hole that penetrates part way into a piece of timber. A hole is drilled for a screw at the base of this hole. This effectively shortens the length of screw you need for fixing a broad timber in place.

Crosshatch
To draw in lines as shading, most frequently used to mark areas that you plan to cut out.

Diagonal
The measurement from corner to corner across a rectangle or square. Both diagonals will be equal in length when a frame is straight.

Dibber
A pointed stick used to make holes for planting or sowing seed.

Dowel
Lengths of circular cross-section timber, which fit into drilled holes to make pegs or secure joints.

Drill
A tool for making holes but also the term for a shallow depression where seeds can be sown.

Earth up
To pile soil or compost round the stems of plants as they grow. Used with potato plants to stop the tubers turning green. Also used for cucumbers and melons to encourage new root growth.

Galvanised
Steel or iron components, such as screws and nails, coated with zinc to prevent them from rusting.

Harden off
The process of slowly acclimatising plants to growing in lower temperatures than those in which they have been raised. This process can take several days or weeks.

Hardwood and softwood
Hardwood usually refers to broadleaf trees. The timber tends to be denser and more durable than 'softwoods', such as pine and spruce, but it is often more expensive too.

Hotbed
A garden bed that relies on rotting manure to generate heat and create a warm growing environment.

Kerf
The thin line of wood that is cut away by the action of a saw blade.

Leafmould
The fine silky material formed when leaves slowly break down. It makes a great soil conditioner.

MDF
Medium density fibreboard is a sheet material made from compressed wood fibres.

Obelisk
An upright column or pillar used in this context to support climbing plants, such as beans.

Plywood
Sheet material made with thin layers of timber glued together. The grain in each layer runs at 90 degrees to adjacent layers, increasing the strength and resistance to splitting.

pH
A measure of acidity and alkalinity.

Potager
An ornamental vegetable or kitchen garden often combining flowers, fruit, herbs and vegetables.

Straight-edge
A ruler or piece of timber that a straight line can be drawn against.

Template
A pattern or guide.

Vice
A holding device often fitted to the edge of a workbench used to secure pieces of timber or other materials.

Index

Page numbers in *italics* indicate a caption to an illustration; those in **bold** indicate a boxed entry.

Acknowledgements

Many thanks to Zia, Becky and Helen for doing such excellent editorial and design work on this book, and for helping to make it what it is. Also, thank you to proofreader Sarah Zadoorian for her attention to detail. A great team!

Thanks are due to Steve Ott and *Kitchen Garden* magazine for publishing earlier versions of many of these projects. Thanks too to Sam and Anna who helped to make and photograph some really useful things.

NOTES ON THE PHOTOGRAPHY

The photographs were taken using Olympus E-system and OM-D system cameras, and processed in Adobe Photoshop Lightroom. The principal lenses used were the ZD 14-54 f2.8-3.5; M.Zuiko12-50 f4.5-6.7, 12-40 f2.8 PRO and 60mm f2.0 macro. Ben can be found online at bensonrussell.com, on Facebook at Ben Russell - Photographer, and he tweets as @bensonrussell.

Ben Russell's photography and photography training are supported by Olympus.